GW01246996

THE PHOENIX STRATEGY

written by
Ian Barratt and Amanda Robinson

Get the Life that YOU Want!

AMANDA ROBINSON PUBLISHING
www.pag-i-nation.co.uk

The Phoenix Strategy

To our loved ones that have supported us, everyone who has contributed, our friends for the encouragement and clients who have waited patiently-
THANK YOU.

AMANDA ROBINSON PUBLISHING
Suite 365, 10 Great Russell Street,
London WC1B 3BQ.
www.pag-i-nation.co.uk

www.thephoenixstrategy.co.uk

First Edition 2010.

ISBN 978-0-9565109-0-7

Introduction to the Phoenix Strategy

Amanda: My main hope from contributing to this book is that people can see they are not alone in their feelings. Each person is unique, but we often have similar experiences and can find empathy in the most unusual places, such as a book.

The Phoenix Strategy is a joint effort, written by myself and Ian. I provide a lay perspective and introduce methods that I have tried and tested to cope with stress and deal with depression, while Ian provides a professional perspective and gives guidance throughout.

The book covers a wide range of topics, from bereavement to how to reassess your career. The exercises can be done whenever you wish and there are tips throughout which we hope will help in today's manic world.

Ian: When I was asked by Amanda to co-write this book, my aim was to provide an insight into what can cause stress and depression in us all and to be able to give something back to those people who may need help. In my time as a stress management consultant, I have found that there are never two situations alike, but using the tools and techniques which we describe in this book, there is the opportunity to develop your emotional and physical well being.

If this type of book had been available when I was at my lowest point a few years ago, it would have been very different for me. I've referred to the book as a 'self-help bible,' but it is more than that; it empowers individuals to make choices in most aspects of their lives and work towards having the life they wish.

The Phoenix Strategy: Use the negatives to build experience and rise from the ashes and enjoy your flight into the life that you want to have.

Affirmation: I believe I can achieve!

How to use this book:

Amanda: Throughout this book, Ian and I will introduce ways to deal with a variety of topics; including career choices, stress, depression, anxiety, goal setting and dreams. We will comment where we feel appropriate and illustrate, where possible, with the use of case studies.

You can choose to read the book cover to cover or pick and choose exercises to do or sections to read. This book, after all, was written for you, so use it as, how and when you wish.

Exercises can be found in white boxes:

> EXAMPLE:
> **EXERCISE 1:**
> Written in each example will be what to do, how to do it and there will be space to write in the book. Alternatively, you can use separate piece of paper or a notebook.

Case studies are clearly marked 'case study' and in bold:

EXAMPLE:
Case Study 1:

Everyone who is referred to in the case studies have agreed to this publication.

Commentary will be introduced with 'Amanda' [lay perspective] or 'Ian' [professional].

Tips are enclosed in blue boxes so they are easy to identify:

TIPS
They assist to reinforce the points made. If you do not have time to read the whole chapter, you can always read the tips.

At the end of each chapter is an affirmation, which you can copy onto cards if you wish to.

We hope you enjoy engaging with the Phoenix Strategy and that it brings the same joys into your life as it has into ours.

Amanda and Ian

Chapter 1: Analyser:

Amanda: Analysing this moment, the 'now,' can help you gain acceptance of the situation or the pain that you are experiencing and lead you towards a brighter future. When I have difficulty or suffer stress, I regard the experience as the 'now,' 'this week,' or even 'this year'.

When you are able to recognise that a negative period in your life is just part of your life, you will be able to identify that there are happy periods too. Whatever you want, is yours waiting for you to go for it. I know how difficult it is to feel positive in the low times, but if you can recall that the last period of unhappiness was followed by happy events, then you are on the way to understanding unhappiness as a period of time.

EXERCISE 1: ANALYSER	
How do you feel	
Why?	

How long have you felt like this?	
Has there been an event which triggered the feeling?	
How would you like to feel?	
What would produce that feeling?	
Have you felt like that before?	

Is the way to get what you want within your control?	
What is stopping you?	

Now let us work together on the questions.
How do you feel?
It is good to check how you feel from time to time. There is guidance by Ian on how to keep a stress diary on page 17.

Why?
If you are able to recognise what triggers an emotion, it is more within your control. Once you are able to do this, you can use the triggers to produce the emotions that you want.

How long have you felt like this?
If you have felt unhappy for a significant period, you should consider a visit to your GP. For example, when I had cried 11 hours one day I knew it was a signal to ask for help.

Has there been a major event?

If there has, you may wish to discuss it with your GP, contact a counselling service or talk to a good friend.
How would you like to feel?
I think most of us would say 'happy,' but what about confident, self-assured, content, attractive, sexy, loved, wanted, desired, needed, young, mature, in love, free, alone, etc.

Try writing down everything that comes to mind here:

I want to feel...

Once you are able to see how you want to feel, you are more likely to achieve it.

Have you felt like that before?
If you have, you can experience the feeling again. If not, do not worry as every feeling was new once.

What would produce that feeling?

It could be money, security, love, laughter, romance, family, friends. If you said love or money for example, look behind that and ask yourself whether it is more than that, perhaps security?
Is the way to get what you want within your control?
If it would help to have more security, can you increase your income, for example? If what you want is within your control, then the way forward is clear. If not then you are likely to need to think things through thoroughly and plan a way forward.

What's stopping you?
If you know what you want, then there is always a way to get it and move towards your goal. We will deal with this in 'Goal Setting and Planning'.

Next, let us try the Happy Exercise:

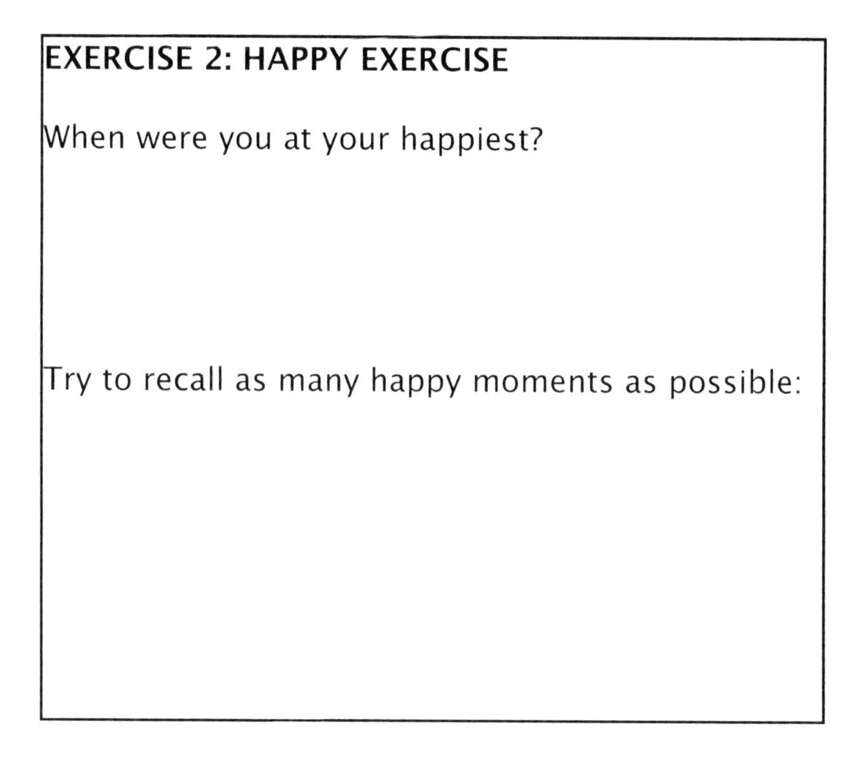

EXERCISE 2: HAPPY EXERCISE

When were you at your happiest?

Try to recall as many happy moments as possible:

Now look at your answers; is there a common connection? Was it the people you were with? First experiences? A means of escape? A time with few worries?

If you want that feeling again, identify the connection and work on making new memories with that. Alternatively, whenever you feel deflated, look at the list you have created and return to that point in time, close your eyes and lose yourself in the joy of it. Throughout the book, we will work on increasing levels of happiness.

Affirmation: I am open to the joys of my life and to receive new happiness into it.

Chapter 2: Stress

Ian: Stress can exhibit itself in many ways, for example:
Sleeplessness
Lethargy
Anxiety
Poor performance at work
Loss of self-esteem
Confidence drop
Excess use of caffeine/drugs
Change in diet
Impatience
Effect on libido
Irritability

I coach a wide variety of people who demonstrate many different ways of dealing with stressful situations. Some appear to be very calm on the outside which can often mean that they are hiding all manner of problems, while others are more open in terms of what they want to discuss, or their body language tells all. The fact is that we are all different when it comes to how we cope with stress and some people thrive on it, often ignoring the damage that it might be causing them.

Some of the outward signs of stress are easier to spot, such as mood swings, anger and breathing difficulties. However, there are other symptoms of stress which are more difficult to spot such as high blood pressure, ulcers and heart problems.

These are some of the most common symptoms of stress:
Headaches

Migraines
Nausea
Asthma
Anxiety attacks
Breathing difficulties
Fatigue
Lack of self esteem
Unnecessary worrying
Irritable bowel syndrome
Negativity
Depression
Mental health problems
Anger and aggression
Aches and pains
Forgetfulness
Insomnia
Heart problems
Strokes
Addictions

People often turn to drinking alcohol or smoking, both of which have a temporary feel good factor about them and make you think that the problems you had were not quite so bad. These types of coping strategies are defined as unhealthy rather than healthy.

The Stress Diary should be your starting point to help you identify where your stress problems may lie. In turn, this will help you think about the ways that you cope with stress and will provide a benchmark for future actions.

The Stress Diary
If you are feeling stressed, you may not be able to identify what exactly is causing the problems, the stress

diary is a really simple way to identify the major stressors in your life. As an easy method of identifying stress, this is about as simple as it gets, but you have to keep it going for a minimum of 2 weeks.

How to keep a Stress Diary

On a piece of paper, or better still a spreadsheet on your computer, mark down hourly time slots down the left of the page and days of the week across the top like so:

Example:

	Mon	Tues	Wed	Thur	Fri	Sat	Sun
8	9						
10	9						
12							
14							
16	7						
18	8						
20							
22							
23							

During the course of the next 2 weeks, your aim is to make a brief note of any stressful situations that occur. You will also need to record what caused the stressful event and how long the discomfort lasted. Also make a note of what you did to relieve the situation, if anything.

Score each stressful event between 1-10. 1 = low, 10 = high. It's probably only worth highlighting those situations where you score over 5 unless there are several low scores that are contributing to the overall problem. Be aware of these.

In our example above, our imaginary stressed person has particularly high stress levels on Monday morning at 8.00am, scoring a 9 out of a possible 10 and again at 10.00am where he scored another 9, at 4pm when he scored 7 and again at 6pm when he scored 8.

By keeping this diary for a further week, he may see some patterns emerging and if the scores repeat themselves or come close, there is certainly some scope for investigating what the causes are. In this example, we will give you some clues to indicate a familiar story. The peaks at 8am and 6pm are the result of travelling to and from work and all the associated stress that goes with that.

The peak in the afternoon at 4pm is the stress caused by worrying if the work he has to finish that day will get done in time. This may repeat itself everyday if the problem is not dealt with. Back to the high score at 10am, this is representative of the first day of the new working week and the realisation of what has to be completed on the day. Not much sign of any coping strategies kicking in here!

So what should you do if you find that there are patterns of stress activity that occur too frequently? Once you have all the evidence, work out what needs to be done as a priority. Never try to deal with all the stressors in one go, you will only make things worse. Bite size chunks always.

Amanda: It is always beneficial to assess how life is going and the stress diary is a good exercise to undertake, even when things are going well.

I would recommend that following this exercise, you keep a simple daily version where you record a +/-or smile or frown, linked to why, in your diary. I do this and it helps me to see when I have been working too hard and reminds me to take a break. It has also helped me to recognise when a relationship has not been working!

Case Study 1: Ian

My marriage was already acrimonious and only heading in one way when I was approached by a company late in 1999. The next few months were very difficult for me as I battled with the disintegrating home life whilst trying to learn the new role which was becoming more demanding by the day. I had not spoken to anyone at work about what was happening, which meant that apart from a few close friends, I had no support network.

I recall the day very vividly when I actually told my boss about why concentration levels had dipped so much and what was going on in my life. He told me he was not interested and that I should start producing the results as that's what I was there to do. I turned round and walked out of the office. I resigned a few weeks later but I was encouraged to stay by my boss, who at last became more understanding. Things began to improve after that.

After consulting with my doctor, things became much clearer. Looking back, I wish I had sought professional help from a stress counsellor as this could have helped me immensely and at a much earlier stage than when I gave up hope.

Ian: There are many different causes of stress and to what level they affect you will depend upon a variety of situations. In the modern world, stress is quite often a combination of work and home. In my experience, this cycle of stress can lead to you never being away from problems that affect you 24/7. If you are reading this and thinking 'that's me,' now is the time to do something about it!

Separating home and work stress will immediately halve the problem. Prioritise your stressors into a list and choose the one that is causing the major issue. If it's your job that's untenable, make plans to update your cv and send it out to recruitment companies and prospective employers as quickly as possible.

As you scan down your list, mark the causes that may be affecting you at this present moment in time. Then, try to put a percentage value next to the cause to identify what you need to focus on first. Remember to deal with each problem at a time in bite size chunks.

A lot of clients that I see have many stressful events to contend with in their lives; some are minor and some are major. There is a famous stress measurement tool, developed by two psychiatrists called Holmes and Rahe in 1967. It is still used today.

To see how you 'rate,' count the units for each event which has happened in the past year.

LIFE EVENT	LIFE CHANGE UNITS
Death of a spouse	100
Divorce	73
Marital separation	65
Imprisonment	63
Death of a close family member	63
Personal injury or illness	53
Marriage	50
Dismissal from work	47
Marital reconciliation	45
Retirement	45
Change in health of family	44
Pregnancy	40
Sexual difficulties	39
Gain a new family member	39

Business readjustment	39
Change in financial state	38
Major mortgage	32
Foreclosure of mortgage or loan	30
Change in work responsibilities	29
Child leaving home	29
Trouble with in-laws	29
Outstanding personal achievement	28
Spouse starts or stops work	26
Begin or end school	26
Change in living conditions	25
Revision of personal habits	24
Trouble with boss	23
Change of working hours or conditions	20
Change in residence	20
Change in schools	20
Change in recreation	19
Change in church activities	19
Change in social activities	18
Minor mortgage or loan	17
Change in sleeping habits	16
Change in number of family	15
Change in eating habits	15
Vacation	13
Christmas	12
Minor violation of law	11

Score of 300+: At risk of illness, seek qualified assistance immediately.
Score between 150-299: Risk of illness moderate, but be aware of warning signs.
Score of 150 or below: Slight risk of illness, but be aware of warning signs.

TIPS

RULE 1 Identify what your stressors are and priotise them
RULE 2 Deal with your stressors one at a time
RULE 3 If you cannot influence or change a situation, try to let it go!
RULE 4 Put things into perspective

The following exercise puts the above tips into practice. Please use a separate sheet of paper for this exercise.

	EXERCISE 3: GOLDEN RULES
Rule 1	Identify what your stressors are and prioritise them. Write down all the things that are causing you stress, no matter how small they may seem. Then separate them into major and minor points and give them values in terms of the order of importance. Score 10 points for high and 1 for low.

Rule 2	Deal with your stressors one at a time. Once you have your list, keep anything that scores 5 or more and discard the others at present. There will likely be up to 4 stressors where you have scored between 5 and 10 points. Put the in an order of priority to reflect how you want to deal with them, the most important first. Deal with each on an individual basis, don't try to fix all the problems at once. Set realistic goals for reducing the stress in a particular area.
Rule 3	If you cannot influence a situation, try to let it go! When preparing your list, you may find that you include some situations where things are outside of your control and you simply can't influence the outcome. Any stressors that fall into this category should be written down on a piece of paper and have a line drawn through them or even better, burn the evidence in a safe and responsible manner. The effect of doing this will be to release those situations that you can't control and enable you to concentrate on the real tasks in hand, the things you can influence and change in your life.

Rule 4	Put things into perspective While all this is going on in your world, take time to reflect on what you have discovered so far. It's important to remember to put all these things into perspective and to ask yourself an important question when you are faced with a stressful challenge: 'What is the worst case scenario?'. Learning how to put things into perspective will help you realise what is important and what you can immediately stop worrying about, leaving you to deal with the other matters which are of high priority.

Amanda: Take each moment step by step. Let every negative aspect go from your life today and wake up tomorrow and start afresh. Each day is a new day. Look forward to tomorrow, next week, next year.

Affirmation: A new day is a blank canvas, which can become whatever you wish.

Chapter 3: Worrying

Ian: The effect of worrying can produce a chemical reaction in your body. When you are scared or in a dangerous position, your body releases adrenalin. This is a result of the 'fight or flight' reflex that evolved to help us to overcome or run away from anything that threatened us physically.

Adrenalin directly affects the digestive system and, as a result, can make you feel ill. The more you worry, the worse it gets and a sudden rush of adrenalin can lead to your stomach churning, a dry mouth, palpitations, a headache, or feeling nauseous.

It can also be very difficult to get to sleep when you worry and this can get worse at night. As you unwind and while you're trying to drop off to sleep there is nothing to distract you from the worries that may have been lurking in the background during the day.

EXERCISE 4: WORRY	
What I am worried about	What actions I can take

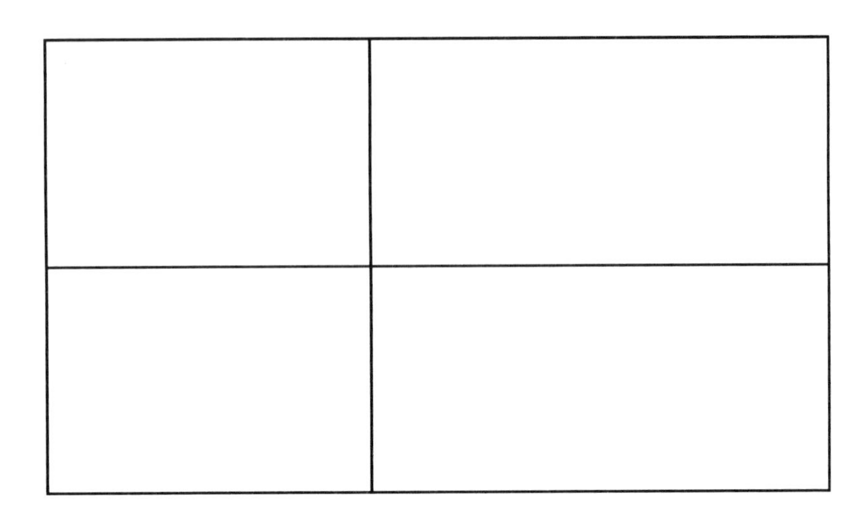

When you have completed the list above, mark the problems in the order that you need to deal with them and then do exactly that. Do not take on more than one problem at a time as this is likely to raise your stress levels more.

If you then gauge your concerns on a scale of 1-10 [10 being the highest], you will probably only need to focus on anything above 5.

It is important that you do not list questions in the first column, but simply statements such as 'I am worried about missing a work deadline'. In the second column, make a note of exactly what you can do to make it happen. If you find that you cannot influence something, remember to let them go as you cannot change the outcome!

If you can, keep this list going for a few weeks, which will give you time to reflect and then refer back to it. You will find that you can cross some things off, either because events you were dreading did not happen or they have shrunk to insignificance.

How to stop worrying:
Worrying can occur if you spend a lot of time thinking negative thoughts and about negative outcomes. For example, you may worry about things you cannot influence, thereby creating additional pressures on top of problems that you can resolve. Also past, present and future concerns can be rolled into one which creates a massive bundle of negative energy that you somehow have to manage.

If you are powerless to change something, learn to let it go and concentrate on situations that you can influence. Ask yourself what the worst case scenario is. You may find this changes your perspective. Remember that once something has happened, there is often nothing you can do to change it.

How to change
It is always a good idea to talk things over with someone who is not directly involved with your life, for example a counsellor or qualified coach could help you arrive at a better understanding of your worries and effects on your stress levels. You can also follow the coping strategies and do the exercises in this book, which should help.

Sleeping problems
I have found that sleep deprivation has been one of the most common reasons for people suffering from stress, anxiety and depression. Insomnia can be particularly

distressing for many people as they just don't know what they can or should do to get a good night's rest.

Sleep is very important for both our physical and mental wellbeing. Losing sleep can bring on bouts of depression and worry. You may also notice signs of behavioural personality changes when the body is deprived of sleep for long periods. Research suggests that the quality of sleep is more important than the quantity.

Affirmation: I am in control of my life and can control my destiny.

Chapter 4: Bereavement

Amanda: I decided that this section should be included because I recall that when I lost my mum, I could not find anything which confirmed what I felt was 'normal,' so I felt isolated.

Bereavement can take many forms; death, the end of a relationship, or the end of a particular period in your life. Reactions to such events are very similar; loss, fear, rush of emotions, panic, loneliness, anger, resentment.

Not everyone can understand because:
They are not you and you are unique.
They did not have the same emotional connection that you did.

In all honesty, grief is dreadful, but unfortunately for us all it is a part of our lives. It can take days, months or years to work through the emotions and I just look at my life without my mum as another chapter.

The main thing I want to say is sorry. I am sorry for your loss. I am sorry for the pain that you are feeling. Life changes when we experience loss. It never is the same, but life gives you different chances and a new path to lead back to happiness.

There are coping strategies in Chapter 6, which can help and I've found that I have used most of these throughout the past six years.

Case Study 2:

I had lost everything. I had nothing. Platitudes about how life would get better merely annoyed me. I had looked for anything which would give me hope, only to see anguish and a heart which oozed pain.

My spark had gone and my hair clung to my head. I was useless. Unwanted. Alone. Not worthy of tomorrow, I begged for the pain to end.

Freedom called me. Would life end?

Amanda: At this point in my life, I felt so distraught and without purpose that I wanted my life to end. When I look at it now and think back, I wanted to feel better and my life as it was to end.

There is something I am going to tell you which may surprise you; a LOT of people have told me that they have wanted to die. A LOT of people have said they wanted to end their lives. Feeling that the only way forward is to end one's life is a natural conclusion when it feels as though there is an endless mountain of pain and we cannot see a way forward.

Bereavement brings a lot of raw emotions to the surface and it is difficult for anyone to cope with. Throughout the time of writing this book, both Ian and I decided that the main thing we needed to offer you was absolute honesty. Bereavement is the death of life as you knew it. As I look at it, the end of a chapter in life and the start of a new one.

I am not going to mislead you and say my life suddenly became better. It did not. My life has been a roller coaster of highs, lows, light, darkness and productivity since my mum died. What I did do was use the coping strategies within this book to set me back on track and use goal setting to re-build my life. It is a work in progress, but then that is what life is. We can all redirect ourselves to end up wherever we wish.

For some, like myself, the grieving process can be a long road. My mum had cancer and was seriously ill from when I was 16. I'd happily got on with life, enjoying the time with my mum, but when she died I had the pain of the loss, the pain of seeing her struggle and debts, arguing relatives and a whole heap more to deal with.

For some people, the grieving period can be a shorter process and the person can experience guilt at getting on with life. Well, please don't. No-one who loved you would ever wish you to be unhappy. They would want to see you smile, laugh and enjoy your life as much as possible.

A lot of this book has been designed to try to assist as much as possible and I hope that you can all learn from the mistakes I feel I have made. I did not ask for help soon enough, I expected to be able to work 7 days a week at full pace without a break for years and I neglected my well being so severely I am ashamed to say I did not eat a cooked meal in my house for about 5 years.

Please go through the book at your own pace and use the exercises to help you as much as possible. Alternatively, you can email me or Ian; the details are at the end of this book.

There are also emergency numbers listed at the end of this book which you can call at any time.

TIPS

Take enough time off
Keep an eye on eating/drinking habits
Find your support network and confide in them
Make time for yourself each day
Allow yourself to experience the pain of the loss in your own time
Give yourself permission to move forward whenever you feel ready

Affirmation : Each day brings new opportunities.

Chapter 5: Depression

Amanda: Whether it is brief, or lasts years, depression changes your perspective and enjoyment of life. I know how debilitating it can be, how days can be dark, followed by flashes of inspiration, only to be floored once again. It is life changing. Once experienced, I personally believe that it enables you to know your limits, both good and bad.

There are many ways to respond; a visit to the GP, therapy, self-help or flow with it.

Many people have told me that once they have emerged at the other side, they have felt that things are clearer and their hope is renewed. A lot of people have said they have a sense of who they are and their capabilities.

There is no doubt that when going through a period of depression, it does feel like [as I so politely put it once] the whole world is shitting on you!

I think it is important for you to know that I have first hand experience of the topics we are covering and, while I am not an expert, I know the highs and lows of life, but I'm still here, usually content. I have used all of the exercises throughout this book and they have helped me.

Depression for me:
Days too long
Skies too grey
Energy level zero
Optimism= pulp
One step forward, 20 back

Bed my best friend
Time my enemy
Desire for chocolate and caffeine= high

I have no doubt you will recognise at least some of the same feelings. Let us try to find a way forward together.

EXERCISE 5: CHANGE

What is the main thing you would like to change?

Family?

Work?

Social?

Health?

Wellbeing?

Home?

Environment?

Outlook?

Amanda: I chose 'environment', because when I undertook this exercise I had returned to my family home, which I had left 10 years previously. My father now resides abroad and my mum died 7 years ago, so I was alone in a practically empty house. The area had deteriorated and I felt most unwelcome due to a number of factors. I literally hated the period that I stayed there.

When we suffer from depression or low mood, generally we do not see the same things that an observer would. When people are suffering from low mood or depression, I would say that the one thing to try to remember is that how you interact with your life and your environment is within your control.

No matter what we wish to change in our lives, we can. Once we identify what is the most important thing to change, we can look at how to start. Try the following exercises to evaluate what life you want.

From the following three exercises, you can identify what you would like [exercise 6], how to get it [exercise 7] and what to start with first [your answer to exercise 5]. You can alter the list whenever you wish and for a long term plan, please see the Goal Setting Chapter.

In the following exercise, identify what you would like your ideal life to be like.

You can either write in the book, or on separate paper.

EXERCISE 6: IDEAL LIFE	
HOME	
RELATIONSHIPS	
WORK	
TRAVEL	
HOBBIES	
HEALTH	
SOCIAL	
OUTLOOK	
ENVIRONMENT	

If you want to, you could try the following exercise. Look back at your 'ideal' list and take 5 items from the list and list them under A below. Then complete the following exercise. Look at the situation now [for example, the things that need to change] and then work out how to do that [C].

EXERCISE 7: A. IDEAL	B. NOW	C. HOW?
1.		
2.		
3.		
4.		
5.		

Different people have different experiences during low mood, but the one thing we often find we have in common is the difficulty we experience when we have to get up on a morning.
If you want to, you could try the following exercise.

EXERCISE 8: WAKE UP

Before you go to bed, decide what you would like your day to be like.

Whether you are going to work or indulging in a duvet day, try to tidy away the mess from the day, so when you awake a least some of your space is clear.

Nothing planned?
If none of the above apply, then clear your environment as much as you can, so you have something to look forward to in the morning.
Plan you day; are you going out? Job hunting? Meeting friends? tv? Reading? Food?

When the alarm sounds, grant yourself five minutes of day dreaming and think about what you would like to do. Then get out of bed and do what you had planned the night before, or what you thought about while day dreaming.

There were a fair few days when this exercise led to my snooze/day dreaming time lasting 2 hours. After a few times, I realised I needed to do something else, so I would recommend:
Arrange to meet a friend
Join a gym and go as early as you can, before lunch
Try to go for a morning walk, for example to get the paper
Write a diary each morning about your dreams
Plan what you would like to do, that day, week, month

Morning coffee at your favourite cafe

There are exercises throughout this book which will help you with different aspects of depression, from anxiety to sleeplessness. If you want to do any of the exercises, you can find the page numbers in the index and do whichever you wish to.

There are also a lot of exercises which may help in Chapter 6: Coping Strategies.

Affirmation: I deserve love and happiness.

Chapter 6: Coping Strategies:

This section has been separated into three sections:
I coping strategies which could potentially be harmful.
II coping strategies which are constructive.
III coping strategies which can be engaged with quickly.

Section I:
Amanda: in this section there are strategies which most people use which, if undertaken in excess, can be potentially harmful. We have decided to include them, as they are often seen as part of everyday life, but can lead to difficulties.

Whatever something else gives you which is external to yourself can be seen as a coping strategy if it eases stress, makes you happier or helps you deal with life. We all indulge to some extent in this, but eventually some people are lucky enough to live happily without external help.

Sometimes we need to engage with coping strategies on a higher frequency than others and there is no doubt that from time to time, even in great times, we all will return to some of the strategies, but through using the exercises and plans in this book, you will develop a strong sense of your own worth which will mean that you rarely need external triggers to engage a particular emotion.

Escapism
Whether it is a drink with friends at the end of a stressful day, or six months of travelling, both are capable of being escapism. There is nothing wrong with escapism, in fact

it is often a great way to release the stresses and strains of life.

As long as there are no ill effects upon your health and well being, there is no reason to be concerned. However, once you have any signal that your health and well being are being affected, then you need to ask yourself [and it is a personal choice] whether you wish to continue.

Decisions about how you want to live your life are within your control.

Another form of escapism is addiction. We are not here to judge and I can certainly understand how people become addicted to alcohol, drugs, anything that gives a high in fact. If your addiction has reached a point where you are changing or your health is being affected, consider whether it is time to ask for help to resolve it.

Both addictions and other forms of escapism give the same thing; occupation, attention, feeling part of a peer group, feeling wanted, desired, reassured, confident.

During the following exercise, you may identify that you are developing or have developed a dependency or addiction. If you wish to change the situation, you can. It is your choice. Sometimes, we need help with our development or to alter our life course. However, it starts with you.

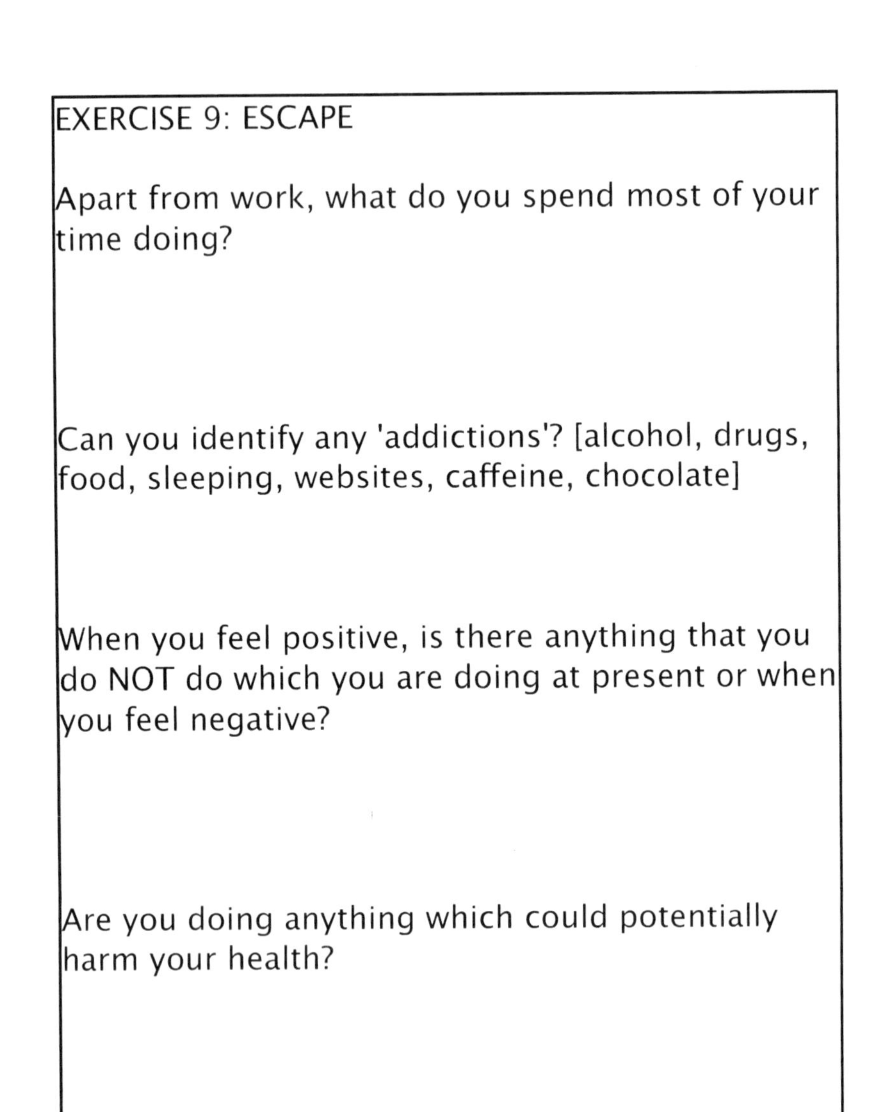

EXERCISE 9: ESCAPE

Apart from work, what do you spend most of your time doing?

Can you identify any 'addictions'? [alcohol, drugs, food, sleeping, websites, caffeine, chocolate]

When you feel positive, is there anything that you do NOT do which you are doing at present or when you feel negative?

Are you doing anything which could potentially harm your health?

If you are concerned and want to change things, you can try one of the plans in chapter 15. There are also coping strategies in the next chapter which you can use to help.

As my doctor once said 'anything done in excess is potentially harmful, even exercise!'.

I conclude therefore, that most things done in moderation are fine. When we are stressed, it is a good idea to check from time to time and you can use the above exercise every couple of weeks if you wish.

<u>Blocking</u>

I did this when my mum died, I spent nearly five years using blocking and it resulted in me having to take three months off and experience horrendous depression. Blocking can help us to cope, to get through things and it can even help us to overcome the stress that we are experiencing at the time by allowing us to feel in control and more 'together' than we would have done. However, if there is an underlying problem [for me it was my mum's death after serious illness for 12 years], blocking delays finding peace with the situation. In other words, blocking is a good coping mechanism, but be aware that if there is something which requires engagement with it, your actions could delay the inevitable.

Blocking techniques include; structure, filling your day, constant entertainment, constantly being occupied in any way.

Blocking which could help put a smile on your face:
Listening to music
Watching your favourite films
Seeing friends
Playing computer games

Other forms of filling your time without putting too much pressure upon yourself can also help you, both by providing a means of distraction and by trying to engage in activities which make you feel better. Examples include; exercise, dining out, evening classes and experimenting with hobbies.

As you can see, all of these activities can be 'blocking' strategies, which in turn can be positive or negative.

Affirmation: My life is my choice.

Chapter 6: Coping Strategies part 2:

Amanda: The following strategies are those which should not harm you, even if done in excess.

They will help you to relax and achieve balance, which will result in a more positive outlook.

Volunteer work:
There can be no doubt that helping others will result in a more confident outlook, even if you experience some negative experiences during the overall experience. Generally, people who volunteer to help others have a good understanding of others' needs and are more open. If this is something you wish to do, I would advise that you only commit yourself at the most to 25% of what you think you have time for. This in turn will mean that you do not overdo it, after all you do need to take care of yourself too.

Other activities which will give you the same feelings are contributing to charities or helping friends. However, if at any time you begin to feel uncomfortable, please reduce the commitment and do one off acts of kindness instead. Remember that holding the door open is as much of an act of kindness as working in a charity.

Art therapy:
Tapping into the creative side of ourselves aids us to rid ourselves of negative emotions. Expression through art or writing helps us to connect to our inner selves and express ourselves without necessarily knowing where it will lead, or where it came from. There is no real expectation and no consequence to these actions.

I have always sketched and painted, but when I was trying to fend off grieving, I bought huge canvasses and painted the most bizarre paintings I have ever done. It helped show me what I was and what I needed. I found that I had painted myself during the grieving period and in another, I painted the roller coaster ride I was experiencing. The most unusual was a giant M&M taking over New York, but that is a whole other book! [Perhaps an indication of how big my chocolate obsession became and my love of NYC.] By using art to express myself, I did and do feel so much relief that I heartily recommend it.

EXERCISE 10: GET CREATIVE

Buy a canvas or an empty sketch pad or book.
Look at it and allow yourself to do whatever comes to mind. A circle, a square, write words as they pop into your head.
Paint your way around the canvas, sketch your favourite scene, write the book you've always wanted to write.

It does not matter if you are not Monet or JK Rowling. There was one time when they were just starting out too, so anything really is possible! What matters is allowing yourself the freedom of expression, even if you do not know what you are expressing.

Other arty ideas include: card making, model building, drama classes, dance classes and music lessons.

You Time:
There is great importance in taking time out from work, family and your day to day life and I neglected to have 'me time' for a long time. I neglected myself. Loving starts with ourselves, so I must not have felt worthy of giving myself anything positive. We all deserve love and must start with ourselves first and then others who enter our lives.

A facial, massage, pedicure, manicure [yes men too!], in fact any indulgence is positive. Even a relaxing bath, with candles and tranquility can be a sanctuary. Doing what you enjoy is a necessity in life, so whether you enjoy the cinema, museums, galleries, live music, food or learning new things, the list is endless. Make sure you give yourself the opportunity to do what you enjoy.

Also, gaming may provide you with an outlet. I often play computer games and find they ease tension and when I have been really down, they have helped to block negative feelings out. They allow you to go away from everyday life for a few minutes [or hours] each day. I also go out with friends and we play various arcade games, which prevents me becoming too isolated.

EXERCISE 11: THE HOME SANCTUARY

When you are alone and will not be disturbed, put all telephones on answer phone and lock the doors.

Run the bath and put relaxing oils or soaks into it. Follow advice for oils.

Light tea lights or candles around the room, so you have enough light to see, but not too much to disturb you. Turn the main lights off. If you wish, put some background music on.

Have your nicest bath towel and robe ready near the bath for when you venture out.

Relax in the bath for as long as you want, but I recommend at least 20 minutes.

If any thoughts other than positive ones or 'how nice is this bath' pop into your head, banish them until afterwards. If you find this difficult, try saying 'this warm, inviting bath will soak away my problems and leave me relaxed and refreshed' as many times as it takes!

When you get out, apply baby oil or a good body lotion.

Diet and Nutrition:
It really is true that a well balanced diet can help maintain a well balanced mind. In fact, certain deficiencies lead to imbalance of the mind. See chapter 7.

Exercise:
Incorporating exercise into your week can assist you to counteract stress and help to alleviate depression. If you do not wish to sign up [and attend] the gym, you could try; walking, dancing, sailing, rowing, cycling, horse riding, fencing, yoga, pilates, running or rollerblading. The list is endless. You could start with a 20 minute walk each day and build upon this.

Support Network/Group:
The people around you who try to understand and offer a friendly ear are likely to be members of your support group. I have found that there are those who say they are with comments such as 'I'll be here for you'; 'you should have called me and I'd have helped,' but in reality have so much going on in their own lives they cannot afford themselves the time to help anyone else [which is not a criticism and does not mean they are not good people].

However, there are those people who will call you out of the blue to double check how you are, those who will cook you dinner once in a while to make sure you know you are loved, those who encourage you to meet them for a coffee so you can chat if you wish, those who support you when you need it. In my experience this is usually a small group of people, some of whom have been through it themselves and know just how bad it all feels. People like these are diamonds; they sparkle with kindness and are difficult to buy! The benefit of a support group is that you can discuss things with them and that in itself helps.

Visualisation:
Visualisation techniques help to alter moods and can assist with relaxation. When you have chance, you could try the following exercise.

EXERCISE 12: VISUALISE

Imagine that there is a blank canvas in front of you. It is 6ft by 6ft. You can close your eyes if it is easier.

On the canvas, there appears a lady, dressed in a long, flowing, white dress. Her hair is long and soft. She smiles, says nothing and walks in front of you, signalling for you to follow her. She is barefoot, so you decide to take your shoes off and walk in bare feet too, following her along a path.

You feel the warm sand beneath your feet.
You look to each side of you and can only see a vast array of many colours; trees, flowers, birds and butterflies. You breathe out and any negativity leaves you immediately.

As you breathe in again, you smell the flowers and feel elated.

The butterflies gently fly in pairs around you, playing their chase games. They are the most beautiful colours you have ever seen; pinks, blues, oranges, reds, turquoise and purple.

The birds sing gently in the background and you see that the lady has stopped just ahead of you.

She gently touches your hand with hers and says 'this is Eden, please visit here whenever you wish. If ever you need my guidance, I am just here, waiting for you to ask'.

She then fades into the distance, while you sit beside a waterfall.

The waterfall gushes pure water and there is a deer sipping from it at the other side. You admire the beauty of the deer, with its strength and grace displayed all at once.

As you sit beside the waterfall, you feel the warmth of the sun and look up to a blue sky. The sky looks clear, bright and endless. It goes on forever.

You sit here for as long as you want and can return to your world whenever you are ready.

New skills:
Learning a new skill can help build confidence and give you an outlet for stress, by engaging in activities which in reality have no consequence upon the rest of your life. Ideas include; cookery courses, language courses, writing courses, computer skills courses, dog training, dancing classes, music lessons. Don't put too much pressure upon yourself though and if you start to feel stressed by doing it, don't!

Yoga:
Yoga is good for all levels of fitness, but it also helps you tap into your deepest emotions. This can be particularly difficult if you are feeling depressed. I have known people cry when they have undertaken certain postures or meditation.
Usually, the teacher will forewarn you of this. Since most people who attend yoga have experienced this themselves, there is no reason to fear this. However, if you do not wish to share the experience you could undertake simple postures at home. A good dvd range are those of Barbara Currie.

There are other forms of disciplines which offer the same experience, for example Pilates. I have limited experience of Pilates, but many people I have spoken to have informed me that they feel the same relief as they do with yoga.

Due to the fact that I started yoga when I was 12 years old, for me when I want to explore, this is the most obvious path.

Another alternative is Tai Chi, which I practiced for about a year. I found it delightful, but the art requires a good teacher and ten years ago they were hard to find.

As yoga is the discipline I follow, I developed a basic exercise to introduce you to the concept.

Please try the following exercise when you have chance:

EXERCISE 13: SIMPLE YOGA

Sit comfortably. You could sit with your legs crossed or kneel down and sit back on your carves, so the top of your feet are face down on the floor.
Alternatively, you could sit in your favourite seat.
Sit with your back as straight as possible.
Place your hands palm upwards on your lap or by your side.
Take one big, deep breath.

Breathe in, closing your eyes and try to imagine a pale yellow light coming towards you.
Breathe out, seeing your stress and worries exit your body.
Breathe in deeper, pale light entering your life.
Breathe out, negativity leaving your body.
Breathe in, pale light entering your body glowing.
Breathe out, negative energy leaves your body.
Breathe in, positive light enters.

Continue until you feel completely relaxed and repeat this exercise whenever you wish.

Meditation:
Many people think of 'ommmm' when they consider meditation, but any type of repetitive, relaxing action will have a similar effect. For example, while washing up you could watch the water and listen to the sound of the water cleansing the pots.

EXERCISE 14: MEDITATION

Either sit comfortably or lay down on the floor [back against the floor, legs down].
Close your eyes.
Breathe in, slowly and deeply.
Breathe out, at the same speed.
Breathe in, slower this time and deeper.
Breathe out at the same speed.

When you have found your maximum capacity for breathing, maintain at the same speed and depth.
Continue this exercise for as long as you can.

Ian:
Breathing:
If you can teach yourself some relaxation and breathing exercises, this will help you to reduce your stress levels in conjunction with other techniques covered in this book. Some of these exercises can be done as preventative measures before you enter a stressful situation (like speaking in front of a large audience) or simply to unwind after a pressurised day. When tensions run high, our breathing becomes faster and shallower. We tend to

breathe from the chest in short intakes rather than the diaphragm. The net result is that if insufficient oxygen reaches the brain, we become even more anxious and concerned, which can result in stress getting out of control.

EXERCISE 15: BREATHING

Close your eyes.
Choose a word or two words as an instruction (e.g. 'let go' or 'calm').
Repeat the words in your mind as you relax.
Concentrate on your chosen word and tune in you breathing.
Take one slow deep breath and hold for 6-8 seconds.
Whilst holding the breath, tense a group of muscles (e.g. face, arms or legs).
As you breathe out, relax the tensed muscles and let go.
Drop your shoulders down to heighten relaxation.
Repeat exercise as much as you need within 3 minutes.

Diaphramic Breathing:

Diaphramic breathing uses the full expansion of the lungs and diaphragm. It is an excellent practice for sufferers of asthma, anxiety/panic attacks, heart palpitations, insomnia, stuttering or digestive problems caused by stress/ nervous tension.

Exercise 16: BREATHE

Inhale deeply into the lower abdomen to a count of 6.
Exhale slowly through the nostrils to the count of 6.
Repeat for up to 20 minutes at one session.

Muscular Relaxation Techniques:
These techniques can help to reduce stress and anxiety. The principle of repetition promotes a positive relaxed response and old patterns of stress will be eased out and replaced by calm.

Please see the exercise on the next page.

EXERCISE 17: DEEP RELAXATION

Lie on your back on a firm surface with a cushion under the knees and a flat pillow under your head. Close your eyes.
Inhale deeply through the nose and point toes down sharply. Hold the breath and the toes stretched for a count of 6 seconds.
Then exhale though the mouth, releasing the tension in the feet.
Inhale again, this time pushing the feet upwards and pushing calf muscles to the floor.
Hold the breath again for 6 seconds, exhale through the mouth and relax the calf muscles.
You can then apply the same technique to other parts of the body in sequence.
However, do not attempt to do all in one go, just concentrate on 2 or 3 in one session and repeat each exercise 3 times for maximum effect.

Amanda: As you have probably experienced, these forms of coping strategies can lead to heightened awareness and are relaxing. They can be used whenever you wish and can assist in everyday life.

Affirmation: I deserve time to relax and enjoy my life.

Chapter 6: Coping Strategies

Part 3: Quick fix exercises and 'Get Through the Day'

Amanda:

Get Through the Day:

Sometimes, life becomes harder and harder as we get bogged down with life's turbulent journey. These times can be a one off, the odd say or several days in a row. Quite often, when we feel like this, we need something to get us through the day.

Incorporate the following exercises developed by Ian and myself into your day to help you through it. The following combination of exercises provides an insight into how you can develop a coping strategy from combining the different exercises in the book. I have personally used these strategies when I was suffering from severe depression and they helped.

Before work:

Getting out of bed – see exercise 8: Wake Up.

Start the day with positivity. Try the following exercise in the shower:

EXERCISE 18: SHOWER THERAPY

Make sure that the water is the correct temperature for you and that you will not be disturbed.

Step into the shower, with your head in a position that the water gently touches your head first and then the rest of your body.

As the water touches your head, imagine a bright, pale light coming down with the water.

The light washes down and over you.

Now imagine that it is like sunshine, mixed with water. The sun's rays enter your life and the water cleanses you.

Negative thoughts are washed away with the water, going down the plughole.

The bright light warms you and remains to brighten the rest of the day.

Do this for as long as you wish.

Lunch time:
Even if you feel as though you do not have time for lunch, please do take at least five minutes away from you desk, walk outside in the fresh air and breathe the air in and

out. If you really cannot leave the building, try exercise 12 and visit Eden in your break. Ideally, a pleasant walk outside coupled with a few minutes of people watching from a coffee shop or bench would be ideal.

During the day:
Tension release breath [before meetings/public speaking]:

EXERCISE 19: TENSION RELEASE BREATH

Inhale deeply into the abdomen and extend the abdomen out by pushing the air downwards.

Then hold the breath for 6 seconds.

Exhale, blowing the breath out in short puffs, pulsing the abdomen as you go.

Repeat cycle 3-6 times.

The following exercise, the 5 min breathing routine is great for relieving anxiety, for example before meetings.

EXERCISE 20: 5 MINUTE BREATHING ROUTINE

Sit quietly for five minutes.

Look at the second hand on a clock or watch and count how many times you breathe out in one minute.

If you are stressed, your result is likely to be 8 breaths and upwards.
Repeat the following three times when you wish to, or when your breathing rate is over 8 breaths per minute.

Keep looking at the second hand of your watch.
Breathe in slowly and deeply through your nose.
Breathe out slowly through your mouth.

At the same time, count each out breath during the minute.

Repeat this until your breathing rate is 7 per minute or you feel relaxed.

After work:
A great way to unwind is deep relaxation, exercise 17.

Sleep easy:
See the Tips to help you sleep at the end of chapter 3.

Quick fixes:
Amanda: We all know that sometimes we need to make a decision quickly and the following exercises should assist.

Career or life change:
The following exercise helps you to analyse where you are now and where you have come from, alongside giving you insight into choices you could have made and can still make.

EXERCISE 21: TREE

Draw a tree with as many branches as you wish. The tree represents your life and the roots represent birth.

Along each branch, write choices you have made and had. For example, it might be a career choice. You can go as far back as you wish and deal with as many areas as you wish.

Look closely at what you have written and drawn.

Would you change anything? Can you see how to?

The beauty about this exercise is that it highlights that there are some things we cannot change, some choices we may always ponder, but a way forward from this point onwards to live as you wish.

Can't find an answer?
When you just cannot find anything of use anywhere or need a quick answer, here's a simple way to find it.

EXERCISE 22: Best friend

Think about what is troubling you or what you need an answer to.

Now imagine that your closest friend is telling you in detail the exact same problem. Listen carefully to what they are saying and why they need help.

When they have finished, advise them as you would do if it were really their problem. Note down your advice.

There is your answer.

Don't know what I want:
In all honesty, I go through this on average every 7 years. Being a bit lost, not knowing where I want my immediate future to take me and this is an exercise that has always helped me.

As we have explained, I personally undertook all of the exercises and because I had one of my seven year itches at the time, I truly did not know what I wanted and the following exercise definitely helps.

EXERCISE 23: DON'T KNOW

You have five minutes to write down 40 things you want in your life, without hesitation or questioning 'why'.
Start now!

1
2
3
4
5
6
7
8
9
10
11
12
13
14
15
16
17
18
19
20
21
22
23
24
25
26

27
28
29
30
31
32
33
34
35
36
37
38
39
40

Here's mine:

1. FINANCIAL SECURITY
2. LEARN TO SING
3. SING ON STAGE
4. SCULPT NAKED FIGURES
5. EXHIBIT ART
6. LEARN RUSSIAN
7. LIVE IN PARIS FOR 6 MONTHS
8. LIVE IN NEW YORK FOR A YEAR.
9. ON-LINE AUTHORS SITE
10. EXPAND SOCIAL GROUP
11. SPEAK TO MY FRIENDS AT LEAST ONCE PER MONTH
12. RUN ANOTHER MARATHON, BUT FAST
13. TRAVEL THROUGH INDIA
14. PRODUCE A DANCE DVD
15. LEARN TO TANGO

16. BE A CINEMATOGRAPHER ON A MOVIE ONCE
17. MEET PRINCE OR ARTIST FORMERLY KNOW AS OR WHATEVER HE IS CALLED
18. SALSA
19. VISIT MONGOLIA AGAIN
20. SEE THE NORTHERN LIGHTS
21. SLEEP IN AN IGLOO
22. STROKE A HUSKIE
23. WORK IN SEVEN DIFFERENT COUNTRIES IN MY LIFETIME
24. MASTER MY DOG SO HE STOPS PUSHING ME INTO MUD
25. BE HONEST
26. HAVE MY CHILDREN'S BOOKS PUBLISHED
27. MAKE SURE PS FINDS ITS WAY TO PEOPLE
28. GET FIT AGAIN
29. GET HEALTH SORTED
30. GO TO DODGY PLACES IN BANGKOK FOR SHOCK FACTOR
31. WATCH ICE HOCKEY LIVE
32. PRESENT A TV PROGRAMME
33. APPEAR ON MORNING TV
34. MEET THE QUEEN
35. HAVE AN AMAZING LOVE RELATIONSHIP THAT LASTS FOR AT LEAST 10 YEARS!
36. BE IN A MOVIE WITH GERARD DEPARDIEU [MY HERO!]
37. HAVE A CONVERSATION WITH STEPHANIE BEECHAM
38. SNOG KEANU REEVES
39. DANCE WEEKLY
40. BE HAPPY

Number 41 would have been 'learn to get over public embarrassment at noting down number 38..'. Come on, I can dream and not ALL of the list HAS to be completed. Though, I certainly think I should try very hard and set a good example.

While quick fixes do help and do highlight goals that we may not have realised we had, when you get chance you could try the goal setting and planning chapter. The exercises in that chapter provide more in depth self analysis which helps us to focus and move forward.

Affirmation: I can deal with what life throws in my path.

Chapter 7: Well Being

Ian: A well balanced diet can improve your circulation, strengthen your immune system, give you more energy and generally improve your fitness. All of these combined will help you cope better with the stresses and strains in life.

There is no doubt that a healthy body breeds a healthy mind and the food we eat gives us nourishment and vitality to live a balanced lifestyle.

Natural, unprocessed foods contain more essential vitamins and minerals to build and maintain healthy body tissue, blood, muscles, organs and bone formation. How your brain functions is directly related to how you absorb the nutrients from the food eaten.

Good:
Fresh fish
Poultry
Grains [brown rice, wholemeal bread, wholemeal pasta]
Fresh fruits
Salads
Vegetables
Baked beans, kidney beans, lentils
Fruit juices
Water
Herbal teas

Not so good:
All of the following foods carry warning signs if eaten in excess.
Red meat

Fatty meats
Saturated fats
Deep fried food
Starchy food
Sugary, fizzy drinks
Caffeine
Processed foods

These over stimulate or destroy our natural digestive juices creating acidity and imbalance in the stomach, liver, spleen, kidneys and colon. This can cause stress in the biochemistry of the body which affects us mentally, leading to anxiety and other stress related disorders.

In times of stress, we may turn to comfort foods to help us through difficult times. Generally speaking, these are usually high in calories, sugar, salt or fat and are likely to give us a temporary 'rush.' Over time, the overall effects can be detrimental to our health. Fast food, something many of us turn to during times of stress, contain the elements which can cause or prolong stress. While convenient and satisfying, if enjoyed frequently they may add to our problems.

Focus on caffeine:
How many of us take tea and coffee as part of daily life for granted? Did you know that the recommended maximum intake of caffeine is equivalent to 3 cups per day?

Caffeine is found in a growing number of foods, including tea, coffee, energy drinks, chocolate and even some medicines.

Health Effects:

For healthy adults, a small amount of caffeine may have positive effects, such as increased alertness or ability to concentrate. However, some people are more sensitive to caffeine. For them, a small amount could cause insomnia, headaches, irritability and nervousness. There have been many studies over the years dealing with caffeine and our health. Some of the potential adverse effects of caffeine can be found in such areas as:

- General toxicity (muscle tremors, nausea, irritability)
- Cardiovascular effects (e.g heart rate, cholesterol, blood pressure)
- Effects on calcium balance and bone health (e.g bone density, risk of fractures)
- Potential links to cancer
- Effects on reproduction (male and female fertility, birth weight)

However, as we have already mentioned, everything in moderation should be fine-it's when things spiral out of control that problems will set in. If you are concerned about caffeine intake, make a note of daily consumption and set yourself some targets to replace it with water instead.

Focus on water:

Water is necessary for our bodies to operate efficiently. It is vital to control things like regulating our temperatures, aiding circulation and ensuring that we remain alert, aware and can think clearly. Stress, alcohol and caffeine can all influence the amount of water that our bodies lose during the day.

If you want an easy way to check you have an adequate intake of water, take a look at the colour of your urine. The lighter and more watery it is, the more likely you are well hydrated. The darker it is, the more likely you need to look at your water intake.

Exercise:
The importance of exercise cannot be underestimated, no matter how it is taken. Even if you cannot bear the thought of joining a gym, at least try to walk 20 minutes each day. I have known many people who have joined the gym and hardly ever used it. If you commit to a gym, then if you do not attend on a regular basis, you will not achieve what you set out to do.

If the gym is not your scene, there are plenty of other choices, such as swimming, walking, badminton, yoga, pilates, running, jogging, cycling, dancing. If you start by doing 45-60 minutes, 3-4 times per week, you will notice the improvements almost immediately.

Amanda: Or buy a wii fit :-)

Ian: Also undertaking some form of relaxation exercise is beneficial. The benefit of proper relaxation exercises can be immediate:

Blood pressure is lowered
Tension in the muscles decreases
Flow of blood to the organs and muscles decreases
Heartbeat slows down
The body's demand for oxygen is reduced
Natural production of cortisone is lessened

Brain begins to slow down, registering alpha and theta waves (this influences the endocrine system to produce its own natural sedative and relaxants)

Amanda: I devised the following exercise to try to prove that I was eating healthily. Unfortunately, it just highlighted how unhealthy I was being; cakes and chocolate everyday, at least four coffees each day and hardly any fruit or vegetables. It's a good exercise to do every one to two months just to highlight what we are eating.

EXERCISE 24: FOOD/DRINK DIARY

Daily, for one week, note the following:
How many types of fruit/veg did you eat?

How many caffeinated drinks did you drink?

How many glasses of water did you drink?

How glasses of alcohol or bottles of alcohol did you drink?

What was your main meal today?

How many treats did you eat [crisps/chocolate/cakes/biscuits]?

Any exercise today?

Remember that Ian and I are not trying to tell you what to eat or drink, but give you guidance on the what we should all try to aim for. I know myself that I am not perfect, but I am eating healthier after doing the above exercise.

No doubt you have heard that we should aim for at least 8 glasses of water per day and 5 portions of fruit and vegetables. My way, the cheat's way, is to drink herbal teas for water consumption and have a smoothie to ensure I'm close to the 5 a day.

Affirmation: I want to be as healthy as I wish, but strawberries dipped in chocolate once in a while never hurt anyone!

Chapter 8: Therapy

Amanda: My parents and most of their friends were psychiatric nurses, so my approach to mental health is somewhat different to most people that I meet. While there still appears to be some stigma attached to admitting having an emotional problem, there are a growing number of people who recognise the links between emotional and physical wellbeing.

In my view therapies can be compared to shoes; sometimes they are just the perfect fit and other times, you have to switch or even start on a different day. Most people find a dip in their mood once they begin a therapy, so do not expect to feel instantly better. However, I believe that if you do not feel comfortable with your therapist or the type of therapy, your life is yours and you can change it.

People sometimes find that different therapies are needed and sometimes people need different types of therapy at different times. I would encourage you to see emotional issues as any other ailment. For example if you had back pain, you may have to have physiotherapy, medication, heat therapy and so forth. Our emotional health may need different assistance at different times.

Ian: The following therapies are the main ones which are used:

Cognitive Behavioural Therapy [CBT] is a popular approach to counselling and psychotherapy. CBT can help you to change the way you think about certain situations [the 'cognitive' part] and what you do about that particular situation or event [the 'behaviour' part]. Any changes that you can make can help you to feel better. The 'therapy' part comes with discussing the 'here and now' problems that you may have.

CBT can help in a variety of different ways and is particularly useful when dealing with Stress, Depression, Loss of Confidence and Anxiety. By using CBT techniques, you can learn how to break down problems into bite size chunks in oder to make them more manageable. Ultimately, you will feel that minor problems have disappeared [or at least been shelved] thereby allowing you more time to focus on major events in your life.

Stress Management Counselling can encompass CBT techniques, but also goes further into history to probe different situations and life events that may still be causing problems. As there are often some deep rooted causes of stress, it is important that everything is discussed at a counselling session so that real causes are established at an early stage.

EXERCISE 25: SELF HELP

On paper, write down 'me' in the centre.

Now write the following, showing the more important ones closer to 'me' and less important ones farther from 'me':

work
love
partner
family
friends
hobbies
colleagues
home
individual people who have a role in your life

Now write down + or - next to each.

Next, note down why it is a + or –.

Look at each again and assess how much time you spend on each. Note down a %, starting at 'me.'

Finally, note down how to improve the link between 'me' and each.

Now, let us work together on this. If you spend little time on yourself [including hobbies], I would advise that this needs to change. You deserve to have time spent on you. If you spend more time on work than on home, you and relationships together, then there may be an imbalance. Do you work too long or too much? If you spend more time with your friends than your partner, you may need to assess why this is and what you have with your friends that you cannot experience with your partner.

Negro-Linguistic programming (NLP) was devised by John Grinder and Richard Bandler in the 1970s. They wanted to develop a personal development programme that really helped people to excel and build on their skills and personal strengths. So, they set about developing a set of tools, techniques and practices that would benefit everyone and NLP was born. NLP is a very powerful discipline that enables people to tap into their own resources and teaches them how to get the best out of themselves. In effect, NLP is a powerful change management tool that can transform the way we think and act.

NLP can be broken down into three main areas:
Neuro covers what we think about
Linguistic refers to the way in which we communicate (both verbal and non-verbal)
Programming is about our patterns of behaviour, essentially, what we do each day

NLP will teach you how to release the areas where you may appear to be stuck in a rut and build on those elements that are strong and form the foundation of your success. This is achieved by focussing on the primary sensory filters which are auditory, linguistic and kinaesthetic. To begin to transform your behaviour, it may be necessary to change some of the old filters and embark on reprogramming some new filters.

By using these techniques, it will become easier to move away from old and sometimes damaging behaviours and replace them with more positive behavioural patterns. As you build on these new filters, you may find that some situations that were troubling you in the past do not bother you anymore. That's because you are gradually being pulled away from negative old behaviours as you begin the education and reprogramming of the new you.

NLP techniques have been widely used in business and can help with things like improving communication, managing change and setting goals. If how we communicate with our clients, colleagues and suppliers is the single most important element to measure the success of our business, then NLP is a toll to consider. Without effective communication we will struggle at both a business and personal level.

To begin to understand how we decipher things sometimes requires additional help. When we were created, no-one gave us a detailed instruction manual and said 'read cover to cover and all will become clear.' By using NLP techniques, you will start to unpick what makes you tick and have more control over your life in general.

Engaging with any type of counselling service is never easy, due to dealing with the emotions that caused the stress in the first place, but with time you will be able to understand those emotions and cope with life.

Affirmation: I am free to explore myself and my emotions.

Chapter 9: Alternative Methods

Amanda: Alternative therapy and methods are not a replacement for traditional medicine, but they can provide an alternative or supplementary means to achieving what you need and want. Please check with your GP whether you can engage in the list of therapies which follow and do flag up any health issues to alternative practitioners.

I personally follow alternative therapy a great deal more than traditional medicine and endorse engaging with the following methods. However, there are many people who it just does not suit. Different therapies will suit different people, so you may find you need to try a few different methods before finding the perfect one for you.

Acupressure:
Acupressure is similar to acupuncture, apart from the latter involves small needles being inserted into the acupoints. These points relate to ailments. I personally prefer acupressure as I did not enjoy the experience of acupuncture. Acupressure relieved a significant amount of pain I was experiencing in my back by the end of one session.

Great for reduction of pain.

Angel Cards:
These are becoming more popular recently and they provide a means of summoning a guardian angel to assist with a particular concern. People use them for guidance and you can either meditate with them, or just concentrate on asking for assistance. You can also use them as affirmations.

Good for confidence and self-belief.

Aura Reading:

Auras, in my understanding, are vibrations responding to us in the environment. People who read auras can interpret what is happening in your life. Mine changes from blues and greens to orange, which is not surprising because I am creative and emotional. People who read them often offer advice and guidance.

Good for recognising what's happening.

Bach Remedies:

Introduced to these when I was 16 [at the time my mum started suffering with cancer], I have found that they assist in the reduction of stress levels. The remedies are homeopathic and cover a wide range of emotional needs. They can be found in most health food stores and are worth a try.

Great for uplifting.

Chakra Healing/ Crystal Healing:

I like to combine chakra and crystal healing, which have a good effect upon my well-being. However, either can be used alone. Chakra healing involves concentrating upon healing a section of the body which requires it and most people use meditation to achieve the results. Crystal healing involves using natural elements and crystals to address health concerns and issues. I often find that if I choose the crystal I am drawn to [without reading the information on it beforehand], I have chosen the correct one for my needs at that time. Combination of these methods involves meditation with the relevant crystal for the relevant ailment or issue. Try a class or individual instruction.

Fantastic for relaxation.

Creative Activities:
Activities such as art therapy, joining a drama group or a dance class have a very positive effect upon you. Sing your heart out, dance yourself shoeless, paint until you're covered in acrylics! Self expression alleviates stress and depression, even if it is a one-off taster session.

Good for fun, relief of stress.

Flotation Tank:
When I have explained this to people before, they look at me as though I had been taken to another planet by a group of aliens. A flotation tank is not a space ship. It is a large capsule [or bath] filled with salt water. In the capsule, you can choose to listen to music, dim the lights or just lay there. They are designed to lower interaction between the environment and your sense. Most people close the capsule so they are enclosed, but you do not have to do this. The effect of the flotation is to realign your spine, reducing back pain and alleviating stress. After 20 minutes of my first session, I felt as though I was floating for days.

Fantastic for stress relief and reduction of back pain.

I-Ching:
The Trigrams and hexagrams look like a series of lines. Each of these represent a meaning. I recently started I-ching readings again and it is a difficult craft to learn. It

took ages to do a reading for a friend, but it was very accurate. An experienced practitioner will be able to give an accurate reading.

Good for assistance with decisions about future paths.

Reflexology:

I'm not sure anyone would wish to touch my feet [especially when I'm attempting to train for marathons], but reflexology achieves good results for people who engage in it. Parts of your feet relate to organs in the body, so the part which is relevant is massaged, relieving the difficulty experienced in the related area.

Untested by either myself or Ian, but I hear it's relaxing!

Reiki:

A reiki practitioner uses their energy to assist with the ailment, whether emotional or physical. It is a technique which promotes healing.

This is very good for relaxation and general well being.

Runes:

Runes are stones with the runic alphabet on. People who are aware of how to read them can give very accurate readings, but please note that runes are not to be played with, they are to be respected. I personally read my runes once every few years.

Good for reading present and future.

St John's Wort:

This is an alternative medicine for people who are

suffering from stress. I have not personally used it, but many people I have spoken with have told me they felt better using St John's Wort. DO follow the instructions carefully though.

Spiritualist:

Let me say that there are some people around who will tell you anything to obtain money in return, these are the people who hurt people who are searching for answers. There are then the group of people who genuinely are gifted and able to communicate with the spirit world, helping you find answers.

I would never recommend seeing a spiritualist if you have suffered a recent bereavement [in terms of the rawness, not period of time] and I would advise against trying to communicate with deceased loved ones who have not been given the time to become at peace with their new environment. A good spiritualist will always help you if they can.

Good for reassurance that our loved ones are safe in the spirit world.

Tarot reading:

My view is that you can engage in tarot reading yourself if you wish, with a good guide and a pack of tarot which you feel connected to. A practitioner will be able to tell you about your past, present and future, depending on what you ask for. Tarot are something which you can treat more light heartedly than other forms of divination and can use with friends.

Great for showing you the options available in your life.

Tea Leaf reading:

I come from a family who can read leaves to predict futures. It doesn't make life easier, but it has sometimes provided many nights of giggles when I was growing up and my mum would put a tea towel on her head to become 'Mystic Mummy.' Reading leaves relies on how one feels towards the images you see, so the interpreter will 'read' the leaves based partly on feelings they experience while holding the cup with the leaves in. If done properly, they are similar to tarot.

Great for reading the future for the next year or two.

Affirmation: I am free to explore the world and the gifts within it.

Chapter 10: Past is a Great Healer

Amanda: For many people the past has been and still remains a painful experience. Many of us bury our past and 'get on with things'. For many, this approach works. For some, blocking helps them continue with life. If you believe that it is too soon or too painful to deal with, move on to the next chapter.

In this chapter, you will identify where the feelings come from and why, facilitating a means of finding resolution. The least you will find is that you will take a step forward.

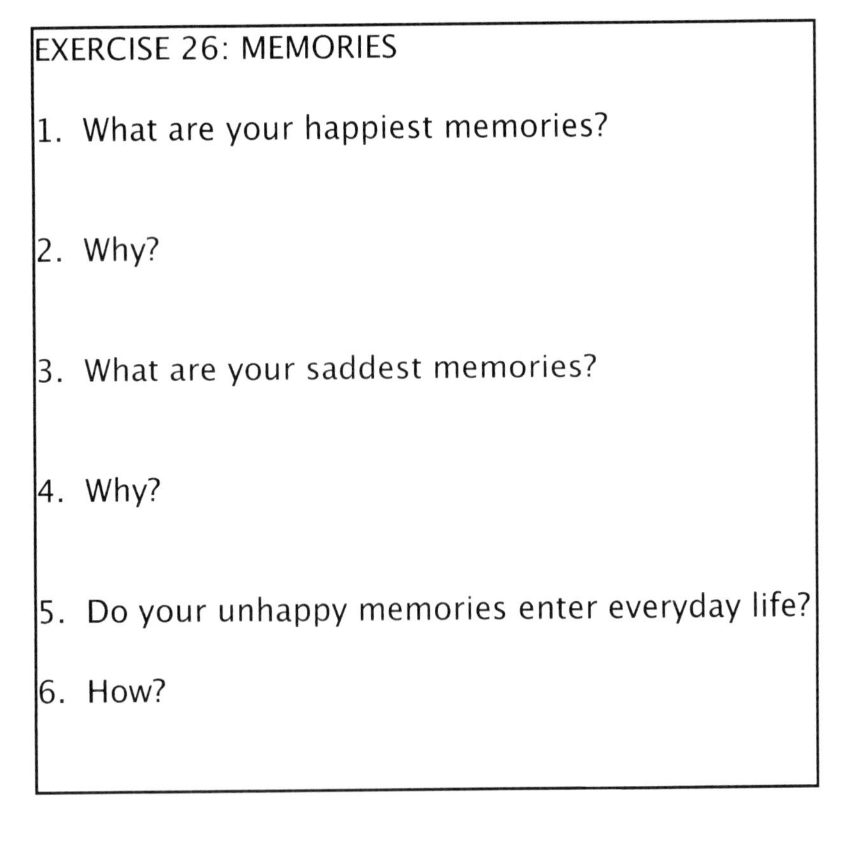

EXERCISE 26: MEMORIES

1. What are your happiest memories?
2. Why?
3. What are your saddest memories?
4. Why?
5. Do your unhappy memories enter everyday life?
6. How?

If at any time you feel uncomfortable, leave this exercise and return to it later.

This exercise will help you to understand what has given you your happiest memories and what has upset you the most. By noting the most positive and most negative aspects, we are able to appreciate what we can approach and heal and what we can move away from, putting them behind us.

The next exercise is particularly helpful for people who have experienced sadness in their childhood, but it can be used by anyone. It can be a painful exercise, but it should help you to take a step forward to rekindling the happy state.

If you do not feel ready to engage with the following exercises, please skip the exercises.

As with any of the exercises throughout the book, you can choose which to do and which to return to, or ignore.

The choice is always yours.

EXERCISE 27: Writing to the Inner Child

This exercise requires you to write, as if you were back at the point in time of your unhappy memory, to yourself as an adult who will give guidance.

Please use a separate sheet of paper and when you have finished both parts and feel ready, rip it up and throw it away.

Let's do this one together:

Dear Miss/Mrs/Mr

I wanted to write to you and ask for your advice.

I am [ ] years old and currently upset/ experiencing pain [please say what feelings you feel as the unhappy you] and need your help.

[Fill in the details, in as much detail as possible.]

I do not know what to do as I feel [insert feelings].

I need a way forward and need your help.

Love [insert your name].

Now, as difficult as it is, experience the feelings you had, the fears, pain, vulnerability and then do the following exercise.
I appreciate that initially this may feel unusual, even weird, but please believe me that it works for a lot of people. There follows a case study below, which may be upsetting. If you do not wish to read it, please feel free to skip to wherever you wish to be.

CASE STUDY 3:

Dear Adult,
I am 11 and my friend's dad got me on my own and pushed me against a wall, started touching me and kissing me. I feel dirty. I could not get away, he was too strong. He kept telling me I was beautiful. 'Beautiful girl' that's all I heard. I kept crying and trying to push him off, but he would not listen. He would not stop. I was scared he would hurt me. I did not like what he did, but he would not listen. My friend's brother came in, pushed their dad off me and walked me home. I'm now scared to play out anymore. I hate myself. I feel sick whenever I think about my friend or her dad. My friend begged me not to tell anyone, but I want to tell my mum. It was all my fault because he liked me.

Love from me.

EXERCISE 28: Response

Dear [name]

Thank you for your letter.

I do hope that I can help you.

[Now explain why the situation which caused the pain arose, seeing the situation objectively.

Explain the reason why there is still pain.

Explain that the younger you is not to blame.

Explain what the way forward is.]

Whatever the future brings, I am always here when you need me.

Just write to me and I will respond.

CASE STUDY 3 continued- Response:

Thank you for trusting me with what happened to you. You are very brave for telling me and I am sorry that this man hurt you.

He had no right to touch you, try to kiss you or sexually assault you. He is a bad person and I am sorry you found that there are some people you cannot trust at such an early age.

It was a traumatic event and maybe you need to talk to someone, if you feel ready. Otherwise, I am always here for you.

There is no wonder you feel scared to play out and sick. The fact you felt as though you could not say anything, that you were keeping a secret, made it worse for you. You have had no-one to console you for the pain you felt. That must have made you feel very isolated. You no doubt also feel that you have to hide yourself from people?

The feelings that you cannot trust anyone are understandable. This man was a disgusting person and it was his nature that caused it, not you. He was trying to use his 'attraction' to you as an excuse for his behaviour to make him feel better for sexually assaulting a child. He is a nasty man and deserves to be imprisoned. There is something very wrong with that man and your friend had no right to ask you not to tell anyone.

Do not allow this man, or your friend for that matter, to destroy the trust that others may earn. The brother who

walked you home showed you that not all men are bad and not all people are unworthy of your trust.

I do think you need to talk to someone about this and how you feel now, but please write whenever you want.

Adult me.

The person who wrote the above case study is now attending counselling, after realising that this event had meant that no matter what a man did to try to gain her trust, it was never good enough. She is making steady steps forward, reporting that some days she feels stronger than others, but is more at ease with dealing with it now.

If you need a break, please take one. It can be a difficult step to address certain issues for any of us and the emotions that flow can be painful. They do lead to relief though, so stick with it.

Another method you can use is the following exercise, which can be used to rid yourself of negative emotions when you have been hurt, or are angry as a result of someone's actions. I would suggest that you use a separate sheet of paper for this exercise. You can tell them what they have done and how it has made you feel.

EXERCISE 29: Write it Out!

Write to the person concerned. Please:
Do not hold back.
Tell them exactly how you feel.
Explain in detail.
Tell them why you are hurt.
Tell them what you think of that and them.
You can also write that you understand or forgive them, but only if you wish to.

Now, read it. Digest. RIP it up!

You can do this as many times as you wish and the beauty of this exercise is that no-one will ever find out!

If you still feel as though you cannot move forward, see Chapter 8.

Time is a great healer, but finding the time and patience for the right time to deal with the pain is hard challenge, but one you can conquer.

Affirmation: 'I am worthy of a future full of sunshine and love. My past is part of my history. The love I am worthy of is part of my future that begins now'.

Chapter 11: Confidence

Amanda: Despite believing that the universe throws quite a bit at me sometimes, I am self assured, open and many people comment on my confidence. I consider that all I have is that I accept who I am; faults as well as the positives and I try to make the best of it.

Ian: The personal SWOT analysis is a great way to identify your own attributes and to help you focus on any weaknesses that you can turn into positives.

On a piece of paper, write down the following headings and spend some time evaluating your own SWOT profile. Once you have done this, ask a close friend to give you an appraisal to see if they match up. You may find that some extra input from a different source is helpful.

Remember to review your SWOT profile on a regular basis to ensure that you remain on top of all changes you may be contemplating making. Using this profile alongside some of the other assessments in this book will help you to put together a powerful self help programme.

EXERCISE 29: SWOT

Strengths:
What are you good at?

What do others see as your key strengths?

Weaknesses:
What could you improve?

What are others likely to see as your weaknesses?

Opportunities:
What good opportunities are open to you?

How can you turn your strengths into opportunities?

Threats:
What threats do your weaknesses expose you to?

What competition do you face? [personal/ business]

The following exercise can be an eye opener and it is recommended that you revisit this exercise from time to time.

EXERCISE 30: Confident?

How confident do you feel?

Score yourself as follows for each of the questions below

0 never   1 infrequently   2 occasionally   3 very often   4 constantly

1. I like to take risks whatever the outcome
2. I rise to challenges
3. I like to learn from something new
4. I set myself goals and stick to them
5. I have my own set of principles and don't allow others to change me
6. I enjoy meeting new people, no matter what the situation
7. I follow my intuition when making decisions
8. I am my own person
9. I spend time every day relaxing
10. I can balance the pressures of home and work life
11. I stick to an exercise programme
12. I benefit from having a spiritual outlet.

TOTAL:

Score over 40
Super confident, you believe you can achieve

Score 30-40
You have demonstrated a high level of confidence

Score 20-30
There are some areas where you are confident and some not so much. Work on the gaps

Score under 20
Your confidence is low, perhaps it has taken a knock recently? Identify the key areas of weakness and begin an action plan immediately.

Amanda: The exercise above will help to provide an insight into how you see yourself. Perception can be affected by a number of things and can be positive or negative, depending on a given time. Also, what others see is often different to how we view and we feel ourselves.

Obstacles to confidence
Ian: Procrastination is one of the biggest obstacles in stopping you from being motivated. If you keep putting off things you should have done yesterday, things will begin to mount up and cause stress and anxiety.

The four causes of procrastination are complacency, avoiding discomfort, fear of failure and emotional barriers.

Complacency, thinking a task may be a lot easier than it really is, can affect us at any time. How many times have you thought 'I can't be bothered' when faced with an unusual or unpleasant task? It's sometimes easier to put off and procrastinate instead of dealing with the issue.

Time management can be the key in these types of situations. If you can prioritise your tasks into those that are important and those that are not so important, you will quickly learn to avoid procrastination as you will be dealing with things in a more methodical way.

Avoiding discomfort can be another obstacle to confidence. No-one likes doing a task that makes them feel uncomfortable. When you have been faced with this type of situation in the past, what has been the outcome?

Has the end result not been as bad as you thought?

We quite often build up a problem into something bigger than it really is and then it turns into a major procrastination issue. When we eventually get around to doing the task, the outcome is not as bad as we thought.

The fear of failure, which is most people's favourite, as no-one likes to fail. This is probably one of the most 'popular' reasons for procrastination.

The fear of failure can mean:

The prospect of not succeeding
Afraid to make mistakes
Believing 'I've failed at this before'
Thinking 'It's a big step, I might not cope'

When you consider that this is not the correct time to do something, you are responding to an emotional barrier. Sometimes, we may feel that our emotional senses are not allowing us to focus on the task in hand and things appear confusing as you can't find a solution. In certain cases, it could be that you are feeling below par and your powers of resilience are low. If you cannot get clarity in these situations in can have an affect on your self confidence and self belief.

If the signs are physical (e.g. you feel unwell) then listen to what your body is telling you.

However, if you feel that it's your emotions kicking in and telling you that any of the following statements to stall your decision on something, challenge your thoughts!
I believe that the time isn't right
I'm waiting for the perfect moment
I'm too tired to do this
I'm not in the mood

If you wait for the perfect moment, it may never arrive!

TIPS

There are several techniques that you can use to boost your confidence. Here are the most important:

- Be self-motivated- your attitude and beliefs will determine the likelihood of success
- Think positively- developing a positive mental attitude is key to achieving your desire
- Be assertive- how best to express your thoughts and feelings
- Set goals and objectives- give yourself something to work towards, then reward your achievement
- Visualise success- visualisation is a powerful tool which can be used to picture success and improve self-confidence
- Lose negative thoughts- when any negativity creeps in it will begin to affect the positive outcome
- Surround yourself with positive people- imagine how you would feel if you surrounded yourself with positive people and how you would feel if you surrounded yourself with negative people constantly
-

Affirmation: I can improve my confidence step by step.

Chapter 12: Self-Esteem

Ian: Many stress-related problems can be made worse by low self-esteem. When you are down and depressed, any issue, no matter how big or small, can have a negative effect on the way you feel.

Having low self-esteem generally means that you have negative thoughts about the outcome of a particular situation, event or even about yourself. Thinking 'I can't do this' is not the same as thinking 'how can I do this?' or 'why can't I do this?'.

If you suffer from low self-esteem, the following will occur if you do not take remedial action:

a. your level of insecurity could be increased
b. you could damage your self-confidence
c. your sensitivity could be increased

By adopting a positive mental attitude you will certainly increase the chances of not suffering from low self-esteem.

One of the most powerful ways you can help yourself to develop a more positive outlook is to take time to revisit you greatest moments in your life- this will have the effect of boosting your self-confidence and dragging you away from the negativity that may exist at this time.

Try the following simple exercise:

EXERCISE 31: Positive Mental Attitude

Take a blank piece of paper and divide it into three columns.

On the left hand side of the page make a list of all of your achievements and milestones, from as far back as you can recall to the present day. These may include: school, college, university, passing your driving test and work achievements. Include anything that has a 'feel good factor' when you recall those happy times.

Once you have your list, start including some reasons in the middle column against your achievements, which indicate what it felt to you at the time in terms of importance to you.

In the last column, put a score against each event on a scale of 1-10, with 1 being the lowest and 10 being the highest. This will tell you exactly what has been important to you over all of the years that you remember.

It will be these achievements and milestones which will form your foundation and will enable you to move away from negative thinking into a more positive, relaxed and controlled way of being.

Just by focussing on what YOU have achieved in your life, things will be put into perspective. It is all too easy to continue to dwell on the negatives that can affect all of our lives on a day to day basis. Teach yourself to lose the negative thoughts and begin to reprogram yourself using these techniques. Don't focus on the negatives, just the positives!

Another way to bring out all your attributes is to make a list of what you are good at. These can be work related, sports, social. The list is endless. Think about your strengths. It is always possible to build upon strengths, even by looking at the weaknesses, to see what you can change or affect. The more you manage to build positives, the less likely you will be to drift back into the murky world of negative thinking.

Boost your self-esteem

Try the following visualisation exercise. Read the following exercise then close your eyes and picture the scene in detail. If someone can read this to you, it will give you a better appreciation of how to use visualisation techniques.

EXERCISE 32: My place in the room

Imagine the following scenario. Bring together a collection of people that you know and admire who have high self-esteem and exude positivity.

These people could be from different walks of life and may be people you have met in the past or some you would like to meet. Place these people in one corner of a large room.

What do you feel?

What are you thinking?

Now visualise that in the other corner of the room there are a number of people who seem be able to diminish people's sense of worth.

These people suffer with negative thoughts and appear to have no positive outlook. Watch this group for a moment.

What do you feel?

What are you thinking?

Some visitors enter the room.

Which group do they seem to go to?

How are they greeted by the group?

Spend a moment observing everyone's verbal and non-verbal behaviour.

Now freeze the scene and imagine that you are walking into the room.

You must position yourself somewhere in relation to the two groups. Carefully choose a spot which would be indicative of your own current self-esteem building capacities.

Describe how you feel.

How are your anxiety levels?
Did you feel challenged or threatened in any way?
What about stress levels?
What, if anything, made you feel comfortable?
What positive thoughts did you have?

Remember that low self-esteem is not based solely on what other people think. You know your strengths and these should be put ahead of any small weaknesses. Think back to school days when other children would be hurtful and wreck your self confidence in one stroke.

Did it bother you for long? Probably not, because it is all part of growing up. Unfortunately, for some people, they never get out of the habit of trying to hurt others; they are modern day bullies! Pity them.

Rise above it all, your strengths far outweigh the odd criticism or jealous remark. Continue to focus on the positives.

During periods of low self-esteem, learn to convert negative thoughts into positive thoughts and positive energy. Write down any problem areas and you will find that the whole situation becomes less threatening on paper. After a while you will find that you can strike off certain problems on your list as they no longer exist.

The next exercise assists in raising self-esteem.

EXERCISE 33: Self-esteem

Using the categories below, list 3 or 4 positive words for each category that good friends would use to describe you. Only choose people who you are close to.

1. As a friend.
2. As a work colleague.
3. As a partner.
4. As a family member.

Then list 3 or 4 positive words to describe how you see yourself as a friend, work colleague, partner and family member and how you would like to be perceived.

Building Self Esteem:
There is a direct relationship between confidence and your self-esteem. This will affect everything from how well you perform in your job to how you feel about yourself and others.

Confidence can swing in either direction quite quickly, depending on the changing circumstances. Being told by your manager that you earned a pay rise through your hard efforts will boost your self-esteem as you know you have performed well. On the other hand, being informed

that you are not getting a pay rise due to lack of performance will damage your confidence.
Gradual setbacks over a period of time (both work and personal) will often take only a small stressful situation to make you snap, a bit like over-tightening a rubber band. You've heard of the straw that broke the camel's back, what might seem like an innocuous situation can result in you reaching the end of your tether.

Be aware of the warning signs and act accordingly.

By practising positive stress management techniques you will be able to overcome a range of emotions in order to develop a positive mental attitude, leading to an improvement in your self-esteem.

There are many different ways to recover after something or someone has dealt you a blow and the exercises which are within this book, in particular this chapter, should assist a great deal.

Affirmation: My self esteem is within my control. No-one else has the power to alter how I feel about myself.

Chapter 13: The Power of Positive Thinking

Amanda: Someone commented a few weeks ago that I always get what I want. I thought about it a while and admitted it was true. It may not happen immediately, but life does provide what I ask for.

Initially I thought is was God answering my prayers, then the gods responding to my desires, then magic producing what I ask for. I have concluded that it could be God, the gods, the universe, the spirit world, or my own subconscious aligning with my desires and producing the results. It does not matter what answers our thoughts or prayers, it matters that we have a chance of living the life we wish to.

Some people believe that we are masters of our own destiny, others that our fate is chosen for us. Both are right; destiny is mapped out and we can alter our paths whenever we choose.

The following exercise will help you to plan your desires and provide an opportunity for God, the gods or the universe to answer your needs.

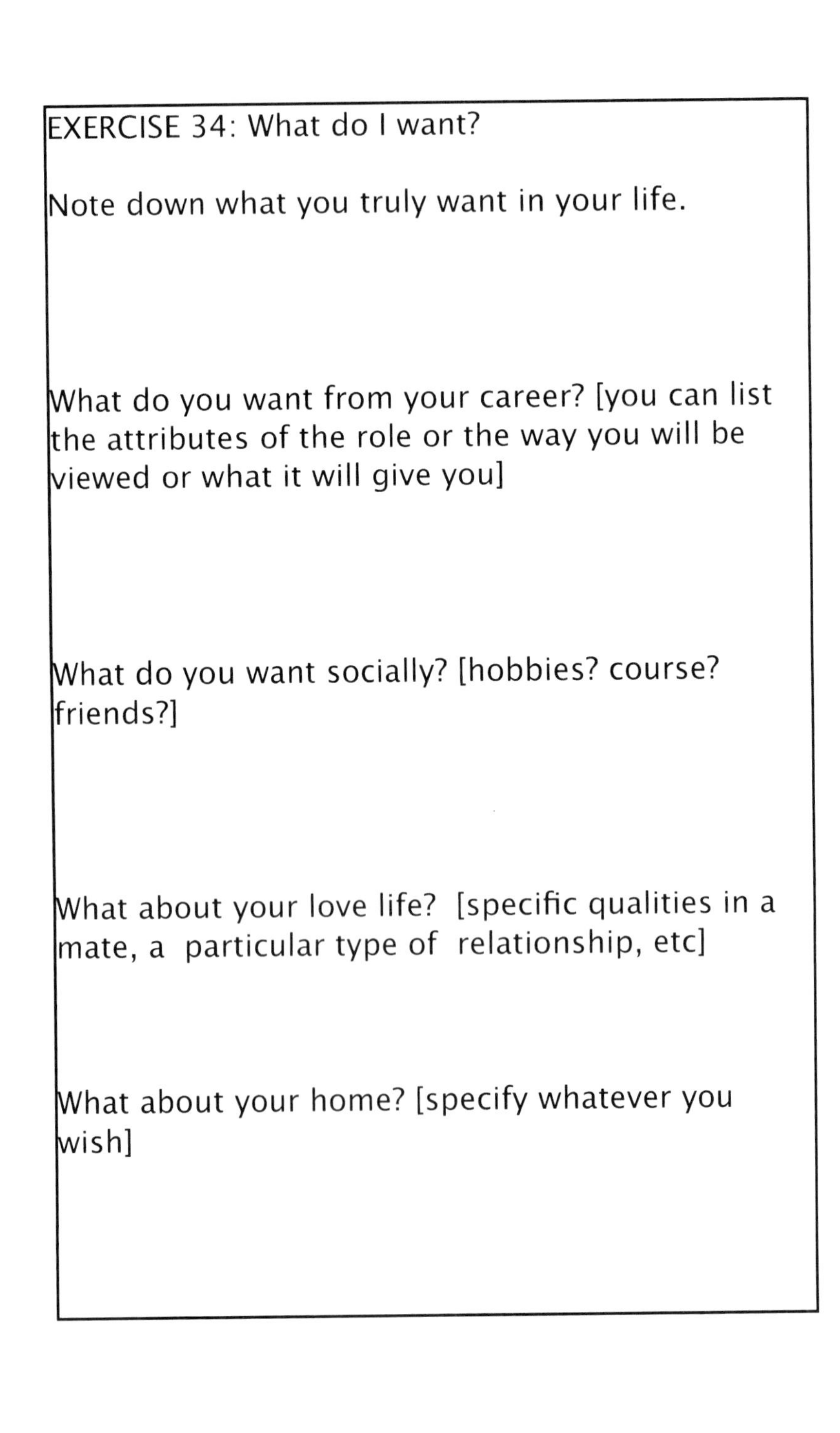
EXERCISE 34: What do I want?

Note down what you truly want in your life.

What do you want from your career? [you can list the attributes of the role or the way you will be viewed or what it will give you]

What do you want socially? [hobbies? course? friends?]

What about your love life? [specific qualities in a mate, a particular type of relationship, etc]

What about your home? [specify whatever you wish]

Visualising:
Once you have thought about and written out what you want, now try visualising having it, as if it were real. Each thing you noted now needs to become part of your reality in your mind. Imagine how you want your life, home, relationships to be and feel them, experience the pleasure of having the life you want. Imagine everything in detail and try to do this as often as possible.

There are many different ways to interact with this and many ways to ensure that you are on the right path to how you wish your life to be.

Alongside visualising what you want, you need to plan how to move towards your dreams. Dreams without any action from you will remain in the dreamworld.

The following case study illustrates that we can use positive thinking to attract whatever we wish into our lives, but we must take some action to move towards our dreams. However, be as accurate as possible in your desires, as you will no doubt get what you wish for.

Here's an example:

Case Study 4:

One evening my friend and I were a little tipsy and talking about our desires. I explained that if you truly wanted something, you would get it.

We decided to note down points about our dream men.

Mine were 'dark hair, romantic, passionate, besotted with me, tanned, muscular, attractive, beautiful eyes, fit, masculine and intelligent'.

My friend drew a man with a, er, large package.

We went out immediately and my friend met her ideal mate that night and within a week I met mine. Unfortunately, the relationship was not lasting as I forgot to include 'sane' and 'respectful'.

If we are confused about what we want, how can we achieve it?! How does God, or the universe know what to send if we change our minds frequently.

The main thing is that positive thinking will be followed by self-esteem and belief in your own abilities, then the magic will follow.

EXERCISE 35: VISION OF BEAUTY

If you are not feeling positive, can you say why?

If you are feeling positive, what has helped this feeling?

Please note it here for future reference.

Whether you feel positive or negative, please try this:

Relax in a comfortable position.
Close your eyes.
Imagine the most beautiful thing you can [person, place, food]
Go towards it, seeing it in closer detail as you get nearer.
See every detail.
Trace the detail with your hand.
Feel your reaction.
Let your heart warm.
Know that each time you close your eyes, the most beautiful thing you can think of is yours.
Spend as much time doing this as you wish.

Visualisation [as above] sometimes does not work for people. There's no fault in that, we just need to work around it and find something more suitable.

EXERCISE 36: FAVOURITE

Whats your favourite piece of music?
Play it.
Listen properly.
Indulge yourself by giving yourself time to dance to it, sing along, or sit back and relax to it.

Did it uplift you?
If it did not, play it again and keep trying!

Our favourite things are usually the things which give us most pleasure. They make us a little happier. Indulging this is usually beneficial.

Now if that did not work, we will not give in! Just think positive, we all have something which triggers the feelings necessary to lift our moods.

It is very difficult when life is kicking you in the teeth to bounce back up and get on with things. How many times have you picked yourself up, just to fall again?

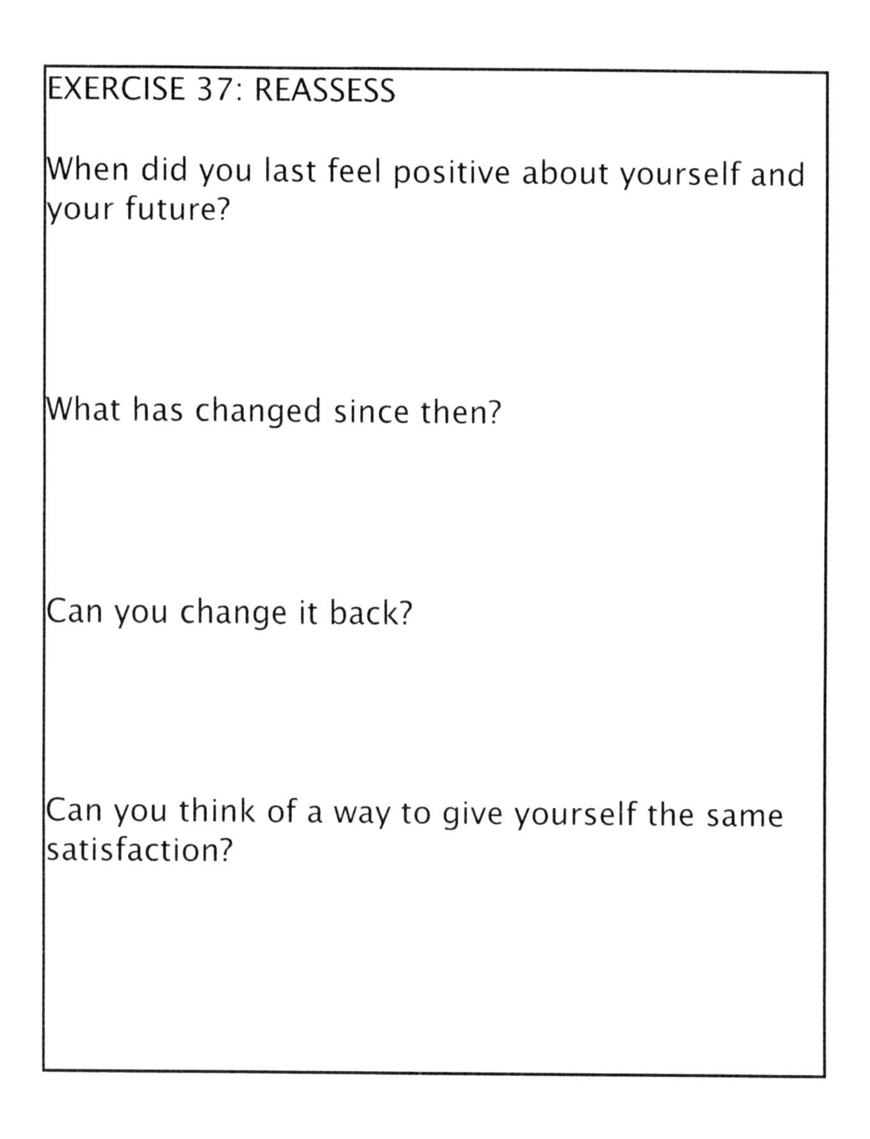
EXERCISE 37: REASSESS

When did you last feel positive about yourself and your future?

What has changed since then?

Can you change it back?

Can you think of a way to give yourself the same satisfaction?

Once you understand what makes you happy or sad, you can use this information to re-frame your day or even your life.

EXERCISE 38: Smile

What makes you smile regardless of what has happened in your day?

Remember that favourite piece of music?

Put the music on, preferably on repeat.

Imagine the thing that makes you smile in as much detail as possible.

Keep practising this and the music will become associated with happy thoughts.

Next time you feel down, use the music to lift you back up.

When we were children, we had no qualms about bouncing up and getting on with it, but over time the knocks get harder and it gets more difficult to pick ourselves up.

I think that the problem comes with experience; when we were children we were fearless, free of burdens or baggage and most of all, full of optimism.

As we grow older, we know that not everything works out as we wish; there's failed relationships, poor business decisions, losing jobs, lack of security and a whole heap of other things. Believe me, I've done it all! Also believe me when I say, I know how hard it is to pick yourself back up, I have struggled a couple of times.

Let us accept that there are some things we cannot change. There are some things we would not want to change. There are regrets we all have. We can learn from so-called 'mistakes'.

Going forward, if we embrace everything we do, it would be more fun than trudging through each day. The choice is yours, but I know which I have chosen. I often still fall [or fail in other people's eyes], I often resemble a yo-yo, but I am more content to bounce up and sometimes enjoy the struggle back.

If you want to be happy, be happy. Tell yourself 'I'm happy', smile and face that world. It's not as bad as we sometimes give it credit for!

Remember that we all make mistakes and have regrets, but you can start to get back on track whenever you are ready and wish to.

EXERCISE 39: Affirmation

Think of everything good in your life:
[friends, home, work, lover]

Think of everything good about yourself:
[kind, friendly, popular, friendly, jovial]

Now copy them onto a separate piece of paper each.

Take these papers/cards with you wherever you go and read them to yourself in the mirror on a morning. Sounds weird, feels odd, works!

You've now got your own affirmations, which will help you with confidence.

Affirmation: My life is my own.

Chapter 14: Dreams

Amanda: In this chapter, we look at manipulating dreams to guide you in your life; how your dreams can show you a way forward and how dreams can come true.

CASE STUDY 5:

When I was 14 my art teacher took a drawing I had done. In it, I was looking into a crystal ball. I had drawn Australia and various creatures around the East Coast. There were sketches of dresses and a few arty things, a town house and water.

While I was travelling a few years ago, I remembered the painting. I was travelling up the East Coast and decided I wanted to change my career. I love art, design and creating. I am also about to move to a townhouse in Greenwich. There was also a large, white house that I used to draw in detail. I often thought it was out of character, since more space than needed never appealed to me, but when I was walking to the townhouse two days ago, I walked past the large white house.

I even look the same as the drawing, which is a shock considering it is 20 years later.

Many people do not understand the power of dreams and dreaming. I believe our dreams give us an indication of where life could go. When can then ignore this, or follow it.

Our brains are much more powerful than we will ever understand and I consider the predictions our brains make [we often refer to deja vu] are exactly that- predictions. They are possibilities, not definites.

Since our brains have the power to show us our destinies, then we have the power to show our brain what we would like the future to be like, in the knowledge that it will then assist us in any way possible to achieve that.

So, in simple terms, whatever you want, if you tell your brain it exists and is yours to have, your brain will help you figure out how to get it.

The most important part of dreaming is allowing yourself to. Remember when you were a child, you dreamed of being a princess or a train driver, you always got your wish! Tap into this energy and watch your dreams come true.

The next exercise should help you to start this process.

EXERCISE 40: DREAMING

Close your eyes [read the rest of this first though!]

Let your mind go blank.

If you cannot do this, imagine a white canvas.

Allow any thoughts to fly in and out as they wish.

Throw away negative thoughts!

Wipe the page clear if stresses or things you must do pop into your head.

Relax.

Day dream.

Let your mind play havoc with the page.

Anything positive, keep!

All else, dump!

Maybe you want to test drive your dream car. What type is it? Engine? Performance?

Or go home to your dream house. Where? What does it look like?

Do this for as long as you wish to.

When you are content your dream world is full of the things you want, open your eyes and scribble the information onto a blank sheet of paper.

Place it somewhere you can look at it as often as possible, add to it when you want and day dream your perfect life closer whenever you get chance.

Dreams are very powerful. Please do not be afraid of letting yourself dream. I know how it feels to fear that things will not happen, but half of the fun is the dreaming and planning!

Affirmation: I trust myself to explore my desires and know when to introduce them into my reality. I believe that I and have the life I dream of.

Chapter 15: Goal Setting and Planning

Amanda: Goal setting can help focus one's mind and, if you wish, block out negative thoughts. It is a way of moving things forward and is often helpful if you feel like life is passing you by or you are stuck in a rut.

EXERCISE 41: GOALS	
MY GOALS	BY [INSERT DATE]
WORK	
RELATIONSHIP	
SOCIAL	
PERSONAL	
LIFE	
HOME	

Sometimes it is not so easy to assess what our goals are or we need to look more closely at them.

You could try the following exercise:
Under each heading, write down what you would like, what you need, what you hope to achieve, when and how.

EXERCISE 42: ACHIEVE

ACHIEVE	HOME	WORK	SELF
WOULD LIKE			
NEED			
HOPE			
WHEN			
HOW			

Another way to set goals for yourself is to plan what you want on a daily, weekly, monthly or annual basis. As you are in control of your life, you can change this as and when you wish to.

EXERCISE 43: LIFE GOALS

GOALS

WITHIN [ ]

WITHIN [ ]

WITHIN [ ]

It helps all of us to focus on what we want different areas of our lives to look like, whether it is immediately or within the next five years.

How many times do our friends say 'I want to be married and have x children within x years' or 'I want to improve my cv and look for [insert type of] post within x years'.

This is all goal setting, but sometimes we forget what we want overall and go along from day to day, then when we take a step back and realise we are off track, we panic about how to get back on track.

The next exercise will help you discover what you want overall and start to put the plan into action.

EXERCISE 44: LIFE PLAN

Let us consider the future.

Plan for the next month:
Work:

Social:

Love/romance/dating:

Hobbies:

Plan for the next year:
Work:

Social:

Love/romance/dating:

Hobbies:

Plan for the next five years:
Work:

Social:

Love/romance/dating:

Hobbies:

The big question is:
What do you want to achieve during your lifetime?

The last part can sometimes be taxing for people, so the easier [but also seems rather morbid] is to write your own obituary.

EXERCISE 45: OBITUARY

What do you want to have done?

Were you a mother/father?

Did you travel?

What about charity?

Career?

Events?

Here's mine:
Amanda Robinson, beloved friend to anyone she met, died with a smile on her face. She was known for being quirky [eccentric]. She was best known for setting up a publishing company which changed the way writers were treated. She prided herself on fairness. She wrote several books herself, including Dancing is My Salvation, the Phoenix Strategy and a series of children's books. She ran 20 marathons, all very slowly for charity and

opened 24 hour cafes, which provided cooking facilities for homeless people. She leaves behind the love of her life, with whom she spent the past 40 years. They never married, as Amanda said she could not decide what dress to wear.

From this, it is clear that I do not mind how I die or when, as long as I have a smile on my face, find the love of my life and never marry! Plus, I do want to make sure AR publishing is fair to people, as well as try my hardest to raise funding for people on the streets.

To do lists:
If I am stressed, I find it helpful to write to do lists and cross off things I do as I go along. I also remember that just because it is on the to do list does not mean I have to punish myself if I do NOT do something.

EXERCISE 46: TO DO	BY	DONE [TICK]

Structure can provide a good means of coping with daily life or depression. Even if it means planning hour by hour, it can help. When you are experiencing times of difficulty, try to set daily and/or weekly goals for yourself, but don't worry if they are not all finished, you have time.

Affirmation: I can achieve whatever I want.

Chapter 16: My Phoenix Strategy

Amanda: The following will help you reflect and digest what you want from life and where you want to be. It is useful to do this, referring back to the relevant exercises and then amalgamating the results here.

At the beginning of the book I felt	Now I feel
Steps that I am going to take	
What I want most	
My relaxation methods are	

My coping strategies are

The best strategy for me is:

My dreams

My support network is

Therapy I may try

My main goal
In a year I will
My strengths are

Now, whenever you feel lost, but do not have the time or maybe the inclination to read through and undertake the exercises, please use this chapter for reference to help you recharge your batteries or provide an instant boost.

Affirmation:
I am in control of my destiny.

A little move away from my overall plan is an adventure, which I relish.

I know where I am heading and look forward to enjoying today and every day.

Chapter 17: Happy Ever After

Amanda: Not quite. Being happy every day would limit your perspective of what is good and bad in life. However, you should be on your way to having more smiles than pain.

How to be happy:
We all need focus, or goals, to provide us with a reason to be here. Often, we can go through our days being oblivious to this, but there are the times when we need to recognise this necessity and embrace it. Structure assists, particularly in times of stress.

A typical day for me is as follows:
Alarm goes off. I put head under the covers and scream 'no, no, no'.
Snooze for five minutes, then realise that I'm quite an odd creature, so bounce out of bed ready to face the day.

Shower visualisation follows, washing positivity into my life.

I walk to work, chatting to people I know.

If I am in a rush, I listen to my favourite song 'I can't take my eyes off of you'.

I arrive at a clear desk. I take a break as soon as I can around lunchtime, walking outside and looking at architecture.

I catch up with friends in the afternoon/evening when things are quieter at work.

At night, I visualise what I want my life to look like, the books I will publish, the people I will help, the love I will give and, of course, the love I hope to receive ;-).

Everyday, you need to tell yourself that you can have a fulfilling life as you deserve that. You are special. You are gifted. You are amazing.

Try to say the following affirmation every day:

The day of the Phoenix can happen any, each and every day.
It was yesterday, it is tomorrow, but most of all it is today. This is MY day.
This is MY month.
This is MY year.
MY LIFE.
I am the master of MY destiny.
Sometimes a passenger may jump on board and veer me off track, or take me somewhere of interest, but I know that if today ends poorly, tomorrow is another day when I shall rise again, dust off the ashes of the day before, smile and go forth, content that I have everything I shall ever need; ME.

Believe it, because it is true.

Best wishes for a successful, happy future,
Amanda and Ian.

Emergency

Samaritans [people who listen]: 08457 90 90 90 [uk]

Email: jo@samaritans.org

CCCS [debt charity]: 0800 138 1111

web: www.cccs.co.uk

Relate: www.relate.org.uk

Email Ian and Amanda at: ask@phoenixstrategy.co.uk

The Authors:

Amanda Robinson is a qualified Barrister, who started writing at a young age, but has only just started putting work forward for publishing. Her first book 'Dancing is My Salvation' was published in 2009, which is travel diary written when she timetabled 'grief' into her diary following the death of her mum. She wanted to write The Phoenix Strategy to try to help people and approached Ian Barratt to help her. Amanda lives in London and runs an on-line authors site [www.pag-i-nation.com] and an online art gallery [www.amandarobinsongallery.com].

Ian Barratt is a Stress Management Consultant who runs Mind Strengths [www.mindstrengths.co.uk] and lives in Kent. This is Ian's first book, but he is an experienced writer in his field. Ian previously worked for blue chip companies in London and New York, but changed career in 2003 and trained as a corporate stress manager.

The website www.thephoenixstrategy.co.uk will be updated on a regular basis and provide information including new exercises and details of where we will be conducting seminars and events. Please visit us.